FOREWORD

by SHERIFF PRINCIPAL GORDON NICHOLSON, QC, SHERIFF
PRINCIPAL OF LOTHIAN AND BORDERS

Small claims procedure has been in existence in Scotland for
barely five years, but in that short space of time it has already, and
perhaps inevitably, thrown up a number of problems, mainly of a
procedural kind. Those in turn have generated a number of
judicial decisions many of which have been reported in the law
reports.

In that situation it is appropriate that a book should now be
written setting out all of the procedures and explaining the ways in
which they have been applied and interpreted by the courts.
Sheriff Kelbie is to be congratulated on having undertaken that
task with enthusiasm and, so far as I can tell, accuracy.

Sheriff Kelbie's book is a true legal textbook in the sense of
having a full citation of authority. At the same time – and as befits a
book about a procedure which is intended to encourage lay partici-
pation – it is written in a clear and, so far as possible, non-technical
style. For that reason it is likely to be accessible not only to judges
and professional lawyers but also to many lay members of the
public who wish to pursue their own cases under small claims
procedure. It can therefore be commended to all who have business in the small claims courts.

Gordon Nicholson

Small Claims Procedure in the Sheriff Court

David Kelbie
Sheriff of Grampian, Highland and Islands
at Aberdeen and Stonehaven

Edinburgh
Butterworths
1994

United Kingdom	Butterworth & Co (Publishers) Ltd, 4 Hill Street, EDINBURGH EH2 3JZ and 88 Kingsway, LONDON WC2B 6AB
Australia	Butterworths, SYDNEY, MELBOURNE, BRISBANE, ADELAIDE, PERTH, CANBERRA and HOBART
Canada	Butterworths Canada Ltd, TORONTO and VANCOUVER
Ireland	Butterworth (Ireland) Ltd, DUBLIN
Malaysia	Malayan Law Journal Sdn Bhd, KUALA LUMPUR
New Zealand	Butterworths of New Zealand Ltd, WELLINGTON and AUCKLAND
Puerto Rico	Butterworth of Puerto Rico, Inc, SAN JUAN
Singapore	Butterworths Asia, SINGAPORE
South Africa	Butterworth Publishers (Pty) Ltd, DURBAN
USA	Butterworth Legal Publishers, CARLSBAD, California; SALEM, New Hampshire

A CIP Catalogue record for this book is available from the British Library.

ISBN 0 406 11710 1

Typeset by Phoenix Photosetting, Chatham, Kent
Printed by Thomson Litho, East Kilbride

PREFACE

The small claims procedure was introduced in the sheriff court to provide a form of action which would be simple, quick, cheap and informal for the recovery of small amounts. There have been very widely differing expectations as to what would happen and reluctance bordering on hostility from some practitioners and sheriffs in operating it. The experience of the writer and information on the operation of the procedure in various jurisdictions lead me to the view that a book dealing particularly with small claims procedure is required, as the extent of the difference from even summary cause procedure is not fully recognised. I have, therefore, tried to make clear the particular requirements of small claims procedure and how it differs from more familiar forms of action.

On the other hand, it is intended that the procedure should be available to litigants representing themselves or represented by lay advisers. They will approach the raising of a small claim from a position of having little or no experience in court procedures. I have, therefore, attempted to write a book that does more than point out the peculiarities of small claims, by covering every aspect of the action which would need to be considered by the litigant, from the questions of who and where to sue through to the difficulties of enforcing the decree once you have it. This inevitably involves the use of legal language and some difficult legal concepts at times, but I have made every attempt to write in fairly easy language, so far as possible, and to provide some illustrations designed to make the book accessible to a lay readership. I hope that it will thus be useful not only to sheriffs and solicitors, but also to the para-legals, representatives of businesses, citizens' advice bureau workers etc and the individual party litigants who regularly appear in the small claims court. They should not be put off by the material in this book, as most small claims are perfectly straightforward and simple, but they should at least be alert to the problems which may arise.

I wish to express my thanks to Sheriff Principal C G B Nicholson, QC, who read the draft and wrote the Foreword, and to Sheriff J P Murphy, Glasgow and Mr J S Doig, Regional Sheriff Clerk for Tayside, Central and Fife, both of whom read the draft in full as it was produced and offered very helpful comments on improvements and the avoidance of errors. The remaining errors are entirely my responsibility. I must also thank my wife for her support despite a lack of companionship during the unexpectedly long time it took to write this book. She has more than a small claim to my affections.

I have attempted to state the law as at 1 April 1994, which seemed the most appropriate date.

David Kelbie
Aberdeen
April 1994

CONTENTS

TABLE OF STATUTES

TABLE OF ORDERS, RULES AND REGULATIONS

TABLE OF CASES

ABBREVIATIONS

Unless otherwise noted, all references to rules are to the Act of Sederunt (Small Claim Rules) 1988, SI 1988/1976, as amended.
SC refers to the Summary Cause Rules – rules in the Schedule to the Act of Sederunt (Summary Cause Rules, Sheriff Court) 1976, SI 1976/476.
OC refers to the Ordinary Cause Rules – rules in Schedule 1 to the Sheriff Courts (Scotland) Act 1907, substituted by Act of Sederunt (Sheriff Court Ordinary Cause Rules) 1993, SI 1993/1956.

Law reports

CMLR	Common Market Law Reports 1962–
D	Dunlop's Session Cases 1838–62
ECR	European Court of Justice Reports 1954–
F	Fraser's Session Cases 1898–1906
GWD	Green's Weekly Digest 1986–
M	Macpherson's Session Cases 1862–73
Macq	Macqueen's House of Lords Reports 1851–65
Mor	Morison's Dictionary of Decisions (Court of Session) 1540–1808
R	Rettie's Session Cases 1873–98
S	Shaw's Session Cases 1821–38
Sh Ct Rep	Sheriff Court Reports in Scottish Law Review
SC	Session Cases 1907–
SCLR	Scottish Civil Law Reports 1987–
SLR	Scottish Law Reporter 1865–1925
SLT	Scots Law Times 1893–1908 (preceded by year and volume number), and 1909– (preceded by year)
SLT (Notes)	Notes of Recent Decisions in Scots Law Times 1946–1981
SLT (Sh Ct)	Sheriff Court Reports in Scots Law Times 1893–
SN	Session Notes 1925–48

1 INTRODUCTION

THE NEED FOR A SMALL CLAIMS PROCEDURE

1.01 The introduction of the present small claims procedure to the sheriff courts in Scotland can be seen as a direct response to the recommendations of the Royal Commission on Legal Services in Scotland (the Hughes Commission) in 1980[1]. The principal recommendation on small claims was that

'There should be a small claims procedure within the sheriff court which is sufficiently simple, cheap, quick and informal to encourage individual litigants to use it themselves without legal representation[2]'.

On the other hand, it was also said that

'Small claims justice should not be seen as second-class justice[3]'.

If justice is seen as the court making the correct decision in fact and in law, then it must be recognised that any procedure which puts a premium on the need to be simple, cheap and quick will compromise justice. All judges would like to think that they have done justice by making the correct decision. Most would acknowledge, however, that it is impossible to be sure of the true facts from the evidence in any case. In most civil cases we settle for the balance of probabilities. Fallibility in making the correct decision on the law is less readily admitted, but, quite apart from any other difficulties, judges are often limited by the submissions and authorities put to them. Cases which come before the courts tend to feature complex issues of fact and law or both. The size of the claim has, of course, no relationship to the complexities. Anxious to make the nearest approximation to the correct decision in both senses, courts prefer procedures which allow for the fullest investigation

---

1 Cmnd 7846 May 1980. 2 Ibid, R 11.1 para 11.21.
3 Ibid, para 11.19.

of the facts and the law. Even where the rules are framed to encourage speedy progress, judges, whatever they may say about it, are not difficult to persuade to allow amendment of pleadings, discharge of diets or adjournment for further evidence or argument in the interests of 'justice'.

1.02 Unfortunately, it has to be recognised that when the claim is for a small amount the expense of a detailed and searching enquiry to arrive at the correct decision may mean that it is not worth the candle. Justice bought at too high a price is no justice at all. In these terms, the adoption of a fair procedure may be as important as the reaching of the correct decision. Justice should then be seen as the peaceful resolution of disputes in the interests of society as a whole, with as much fairness as possible to all sides. In cases of small claims that has to mean reaching a satisfactory decision by a procedure which is simple, cheap and quick, even if the correctness of the decision, in fact or in law, might still be open to question. Attempts to devise such a procedure around the world have provided that there should be no appeal, or only on very restricted grounds, that there should be lay judges, that there should be no legal representation and even that there should be no attempt to apply law, but simply principles of fairness. Rules of pleading and evidence have been departed from, awards of expenses have been denied, judges have been expected to make the enquiries and court staff have been required to carry out work, such as the serving of the action and enforcement of decree.

HISTORY

Justices of the Peace Small Debt Court

1.03 The search for a suitable procedure to deal with small claims has a long history in Scotland. The first attempt was in the Small Debts (Scotland) Act 1795[1], which set up a Justices of the Peace small debt court, later confirmed in the Justices of the Peace Small Debt (Scotland) Act 1825[2]. It is of interest to note that at this

---

1 35 Geo III c 123   2 6 Geo IV c 48.

early stage the court dealing with small claims, meaning claims for
£5 or less, was staffed by lay judges, who were required

'to hear, try and determine, as shall appear to them agreeable to equity and
good conscience'.

Legal representation was prohibited, the defender being cited on
the complaint of the pursuer and the parties being heard *viva voce*.
No pleadings, arguments, minutes or evidence were to be
recorded in writing and there was no appeal of any kind. Even an
action of reduction in the Court of Session was prohibited except
on the ground of malice and oppression on the part of the justices,
and then only if raised within one year of the date of decree.

1.04 Over the years, however, the upper limit of the sheriff small
debt court increased while the Justice of the Peace limit remained at
£5. By the time the Grant Committee[1] reported in 1967, only four
counties had JP small debt courts, still dealing with claims of under
£5, but, as the Report pointed out, in 1965 the Aberdeenshire courts
had had no cases and the courts in the other three counties had only
dealt with a total of 2,200. The Committee recommended against
any revival of the Justice of the Peace small debt court to relieve the
sheriff court of the burden of small claims. It pointed out that there
was already difficulty in getting justices to sit on the bench for small
debt cases, even for the small numbers there were. Only about 1 per
cent of the small debt actions in the sheriff court were defended and
that court processed large numbers of small debt actions quickly
and cheaply. There were, thus, practical and economic arguments
against lay courts and, the Committee said:

'Apart from this, we have reservations about the exercise of civil jurisdiction
by lay magistrates, and we do not think the small debt jurisdiction of the
sheriff court is a matter of trivial importance. We therefore recommend that
the existing small debt jurisdiction of the sheriff court should be left unim-
paired and that no steps should be taken to transfer small debt cases out of the
sheriff courts into the Justice of the Peace small debt courts. The continued
existence of the Justice of the Peace small debt courts is not a matter for us,
but we think the appropriate authorities might consider whether these courts
continue to serve a useful purpose[2].'

The Justice of the Peace small debt court was finally abolished by
the District Courts (Scotland) Act 1975.

1 Report of the Committee on the Sheriff Court (Cmnd 3248) 1967.
2 Ibid, para 197.

Sheriff small debt court

1.05 The Small Debts (Scotland) Act 1825[1] introduced a relatively simple process for recovery of debts of £8 or less in the sheriff court. Unlike the Justice of the Peace small debt court, however, the upper limit was increased over the years and the jurisdiction extended. The Small Debts (Scotland) Act 1829[2] increased the limit to £100 Scots (£8.34). The Small Debts Courts (Scotland) Act 1837[3] reorganised the court but did not change the jurisdiction. The limit was increased to £12 by the Sheriff Courts (Scotland) Act 1853[4] while the Small Debt Amendment (Scotland) Act 1889[5] widened the jurisdiction to include actions for delivery of goods of a value of up to £12. The limit was again increased to £20 by the Sheriff Courts (Scotland) Act 1907[6] and to £50 by the Sheriff Courts (Civil Jurisdiction and Procedure) (Scotland) Act 1963[7]. In addition to providing a simple procedure, which, prior to the 1837 Act, included a prohibition on legal representation or written pleadings of any kind without the leave of the court, the Small Debt Acts severely restricted any right of appeal. There was to be no review of any kind at all except to the High Court of Justiciary

'on grounds of corruption or malice and oppression on the part of the Sheriff, or on such deviations in point of form from the statutory enactments as the court shall think took place wilfully or have prevented substantial justice from having been done, or on incompetency, including defect of jurisdiction of the sheriff[8]'.

Perhaps the fact that the appeal was to the superior criminal court reflected how badly matters had to have gone to justify intervention. The sheriff small debt court was finally abolished by the Sheriff Courts (Scotland) Act 1971[9] which replaced it with the present summary cause.

Summary cause

1.06 The original summary cause was first introduced by the Sheriff Courts (Scotland) Act 1907[6] though that was based on an

1 6 Geo IV c 24.   2 10 Geo IV c 55.   3 1 Vict c 41.
4 16 & 17 Vict c 80.   5 52 & 53 Vict c 26.   6 7 Ed VII c 26.
7 1963 c 22.   8 1 Vict c 41, ss 30, 31.   9 1971 c 58.

earlier process, which it replaced, provided for by the Debts Recovery (Scotland) Act 1867[1]. That had been a summary procedure for recovery of debts of up to £50 in

'actions of debts for house maills, men's ordinaries, servants' fees, merchants' accounts and other the like debts'.

Even in 1867 it was not certain what that covered. The 1907 Act replaced it with a new summary procedure which was extended by the Sheriff Courts (Scotland) Amendment Act 1913[2] to apply to all actions (except those under the Small Debt Acts and the Workmen's Compensation Act) for payment of money not exceeding £50 and all other actions in which the parties either admitted that the value of the action did not exceed £50 or consented at any stage to being tried summarily. The summary cause was, in essence, a variant of the ordinary action but the sheriff had an entirely free hand to order such procedure as he thought requisite. If the evidence was recorded there was an appeal to the sheriff principal on fact and law, but if not, on law only. If the sheriff principal certified the case as suitable there might be an appeal to the Court of Session. The upper limit for this procedure was raised to £250 by the Sheriff Courts (Civil Jurisdiction and Procedure) (Scotland) Act 1963[3]. Strangely, however, the privative jurisdiction of the sheriff court remained at £50, so that it was open to the pursuer to ignore the summary cause procedure and proceed in the Court of Session.

1.07 The Grant Committee[4] made proposals, in 1967, for a new summary procedure to replace both the old summary cause and the small debt court, to apply to a variety of actions, including actions for payment of no more than £250. The Report stated:

'We do not think that the sheriff-substitute should have power to order such procedure as he thinks requisite, as he can in existing summary civil procedure. Instead, there should be a standard summary procedure, which would largely assimilate actions to the existing small debt procedure, and would not resemble ordinary procedure[5].'

The Grant Committee's recommendations came to fruition in the Sheriff Courts (Scotland) Act 1971[6] which provided the basic

---

1 30 & 31 Vict c 96.   **2** 2 & 3 Geo V c 28.   **3** 1963 c 22.
4 Report of the Committee on the Sheriff Court (Cmnd 3248) 1967.
5 Ibid, para 611.   **6** 1971 c 58.

provisions for the present summary cause, replacing both the previous summary cause and the small debt court. The procedure was to apply to actions for up to £250, summary causes could be remitted to the ordinary roll and vice versa and an appeal lay to the sheriff principal on a point of law and from the sheriff principal to the Court of Session if he certified the cause as suitable for such an appeal[1]. The Act also raised the privative jurisdiction of the sheriff court to £250[2] and provided for further increases to be made by Order in Council[3]. In fact, the new summary cause was not introduced until 1 September 1976, when the new rules were ready[4]. On the same date the limit for the summary cause and the privative jurisdiction of the sheriff court was raised to £500[5]. The summary cause limit was raised to £1,000 in 1981[6] and both limits were raised to £1,500 in 1988[7].

The Hughes Commission

1.08 Even by the time the new summary cause came into operation the search for appropriate procedures for small claims had taken on a new complexion with the rise in pressure from consumer groups for a procedure designed for the needs of individuals making complaints in consumer cases. It had always been, and remains, a problem with small claims procedures that they are used, in the vast majority of cases, by large businesses and institutions as a convenient debt collecting agency. The Grant Report, for example, pointed out in 1967, with no noticeable concern for the implications of the statement, that 'only about 1 per cent of small debt actions are defended[8]'. While the summary cause procedure might be suitable enough for businesses which employed a solicitor there was criticism that it did not meet the needs of the

---

1 Sheriff Courts (Scotland) Act 1971, ss 35, 36, 37, 38.
2 Ibid, s 31.   3 Ibid, s 41.
4 Act of Sederunt (Summary Cause Rules, Sheriff Court) 1976, SI 1976/476.
5 Sheriff Courts (Scotland) Act 1971 (Privative Jurisdiction, Etc) Order 1976, SI 1976/900.
6 Sheriff Courts (Scotland) Act 1971 (Summary Cause) Order 1981, SI 1981/842.
7 Sheriff Courts (Scotland) Act 1971 (Privative Jurisdiction and Summary Cause) Order 1988, SI 1988/1993.
8 Cmnd 3248, para 37.

consumer who wished to claim for faulty goods and services in a cheap and simple process.

1.09 It was against that background that the Royal Commission on Legal Services in Scotland, chaired by Lord Hughes, reported in May 1980[1]. The Commission had a wide remit 'to enquire into the law and practice relating to the provision of legal services in Scotland'. The report found considerable dissatisfaction with the summary cause procedure, at least from the point of view of individual consumer litigants, pointing out that:

'The procedure is such that a lawyer's services are virtually essential for certain steps in it, and if a solicitor is employed the outlay can soon exceed the sum claimed. Although the successful pursuer is entitled to recover at least some of his expenses, this is a possibility that even the most confident litigant cannot take for granted. From the evidence we received, and from the further studies we undertook, we believe that there is a need in Scotland for an informal and speedy procedure for settling small claims, facilitating self-representation by the parties to the dispute[2].'

1.10 The search for a suitable procedure for small consumer claims in modern times has not, of course, been confined to Scotland, and the Commission considered evidence from a number of other countries. In particular, they quoted with approval some basic principles which had been formulated by the Economic and Social Committee of the European Economic Community:

'—the procedure should be simple and free of unnecessary formalities; the complainant must be able to bring his case before the judge himself, the complaint being stated by filling in a simple form. Help should be provided in filling in the form, by the court officials, for instance, or a consumer advice centre;

—there should be no obligation to be represented in the proceedings. A ban on the use of lawyers does not, however, seem desirable, in the consumer's interests as well. The financial risk could be limited (precisely because the amount at stake is not great) by not consistently ordering the losing party to pay the other's costs. The consumer should also have the opportunity of being represented by a representative of a consumer organisation:

—it should be possible for the case to be dealt with orally;

—the judge should have great freedom regarding the way in which the proceedings are conducted. This freedom should embrace *inter alia*: the ways

1 Cmnd 7846.   2 Ibid, para 11.1.

in which evidence may be furnished, the interrogation of the parties or witnesses, outlining the proceedings to the parties;

—the costs of the actual proceedings should be very low;

—high costs of expert investigation should be avoided. The judge must weigh the claim against the probable cost of expert opinions and take account of the nature of the product and the financial means of the complainant. The judge should inform the consumer about the costs and offer the possibility of an expert opinion free of charge if the consumer's financial position or other circumstances so warrant[1].'

1.11 In recommending the adoption of a new procedure for small claims the Commission recommended that the new rules should be drafted after consulting consumer and business as well as legal interests and put forward some basic principles of their own:

(i) *Monetary limits*
Any civil case where the amount or value of the claim does not exceed a sum of at least £500 should be covered, regardless of whether the action is for aliment, damages, repayment of a debt or compensation. There ought to be a simple mechanism for raising the top level to maintain its value, by making provision for increases by index-linking.

(ii) *Expenses*
The risk of having to meet the other party's expenses is a major deterrent to both parties to taking part in a small claims action in court. We therefore consider that no expenses should normally be awarded to the successful party, though the sheriff should have discretion to make an exception as regards the travelling expenses of the parties and necessary witnesses.

(iii) *Convenience*
The majority of undefended cases should continue, as under summary cause procedure, to be settled by exchange of papers without any court appearance.

(iv) *Simplicity*
The simplicity of the new procedure should be seen not only in the steps of the procedure itself, but in the language and formalities of the court. The court authorities should enlist the help of consumer organisations and advice agencies in devising summonses, claim forms and so on. We have seen some good examples of simple forms and guides to procedure abroad. The summons should be issued by the sheriff clerk and served by post. This is an essential element in any 'do-it-yourself' system.

---

1 Ibid, para 11.8 quoting European Economic and Social Committee: Study of the Section for Protection of the Environment, Public Health and Consumer Affairs on the use of Judicial and Quasi-Judicial Means of Consumer Protection in the European Community and their Harmonisation: Brussels, 1979, pp 40–41.

(v) *Informality*
Informality should characterise the hearing of a small claim in court just as simplicity should characterise the language and procedures used. It is, however, important to stress that informal procedures do not mean casual justice. The courts must be as firm and effective in hearing small claims as in other areas of the law.

(vi) During our examination of systems elsewhere – particularly in the county courts in England – we have seen the operation of a pre-trial review. This is a preliminary meeting between the judge and the parties at which the judge ascertains the nature of the dispute; he may be able to act to some extent as a conciliator and he can advise the parties as to what evidence will be required and what the procedure will be at the adjudication hearing. We have no doubt that this can be an extremely useful step in procedure. However, we have heard some criticism of the English procedure, namely that the rigid division into two stages – the pre-trial review and the hearing – sometimes involves parties attending twice when, in very simple matters, an adjudication could be achieved at first hearing. We hope that any procedure introduced in Scotland will be sufficiently flexible to enable a case to be disposed of at one hearing if two hearings are not necessary.

(vii) *Scope of the procedure*
The procedure should encompass the full scope of the present summary cause, including actions concerning reparation, aliment and other matrimonial causes, or house tenancy. We rely on the pre-trial review to determine the form which proof should take in each case[1].

Dundee small claims experiment

1.12 In the meantime, in an attempt to explore the needs of consumer and other individual pursuers and how best to meet them, the Scottish Courts Administration set up a small claims adjudication scheme at Dundee Sheriff Court, on an experimental basis, for three years starting on 1 January 1979. The main features of the scheme were that both parties had to agree to having the claim adjudicated in an informal manner by a sheriff, only individuals or, at the sheriff clerk's discretion, small businesses could be a claimant (large businesses might be allowed to make a claim if the defender was refusing to pay because he was dissatisfied with goods or services supplied), strict rules of evidence did not apply, representation other than by a solicitor was allowed, an award of expenses could not exceed £25 and there was no appeal. The

1 Ibid, para 11.21.

Hughes Commission had noted the existence of the scheme but little use had yet been made of it[1]. Only 52 cases were taken over the three years and a full report on the scheme, compared with summary cause cases in Dundee and Aberdeen was issued by the Scottish Office Central Research Unit[2].

1.13 Applying the criteria of simplicity, cheapness, quickness and fairness, the researchers did not find much to choose between the summary cause and the small claims experiment. For the participants in the scheme and for the parties to summary causes the outcomes were equally fair and in straightforward and undisputed cases the level of costs were equally acceptable and the procedures were equally simple. The advantages of the small claims scheme were the upper limit on costs and the fact that the hearings were regarded by the users as simpler than proofs were regarded by parties to summary cause cases. The summary cause, however, was quicker in undisputed cases and its users who were represented found the procedure to be simpler and more convenient for them than the unrepresented users of both summary causes and the small claims procedure. The researchers concluded that since the users of court procedures in disputed cases (and the advice agencies) attached a high importance to the costs and complexity of the hearings, the small claims scheme was more successful for its actual (and potential) users in these cases. However, if the views of the operators were taken into account along with the sheer numbers of undisputed summary cause cases, then neither summary cause nor the small claims scheme had any significant overall advantage. Among the lessons to be learned from the experiment, the researchers pointed out that:

'The underlying spirit of a court-based procedure and the attitude of the Sheriff, court staff and advisers are just as important to the users than [*sic*] the detailed rules. This is in contrast to previous thinking about small claims courts which has been especially concerned with specific aspects of the procedure and the accompanying rules. Also, the people who view the procedure from outside, such as the advice agencies, the press and members of the public, place greater emphasis on the image presented by the procedure and its apparent overall aim than on its detailed features[3].'

1 Ibid, para 11.16–11.18.
2 A Research Based Evaluation of the Dundee Small Claims Experiment by Anne Connor with Barbara Doig. January 1983.
3 Ibid, para 9.7.

THE PRESENT SMALL CLAIMS PROCEDURE

The statutory basis

1.14 Following on the Dundee experiment and the CRU Report thereon, the Lord Advocate issued a Consultation paper in July 1984 and considered numerous responses from a wide variety of interested bodies. The salient points of the proposals in the Consultation Paper were that each defended case would go to a Preliminary Hearing. If the sheriff decided that he could dispose of the matter at that stage there would be no need for further procedure. If it was necessary to proceed further, however, the sheriff would decide whether to send the case to an informal adjudication or to a formal proof. There would be an appeal to the Sheriff Principal only on the exceptional grounds of harshness or oppression. The new proposals would require both statutory changes and changes in the Sheriff Court Rules. The statutory basis for the new small claims procedure was eventually provided by s 18 of the Law Reform (Miscellaneous Provisions) (Scotland) Act 1985[1]. The provisions took the form of amendments to the Sheriff Courts (Scotland) Act 1971[2]. The new small claim was to be a form of the summary cause procedure to be used for the purposes prescribed by the Lord Advocate by order affirmed by a resolution of each House of Parliament[3]. The Lord Advocate is also required to prescribe by such an order a value of claim below which no award of expenses may be made and a maximum sum of expenses which may be awarded in any other case. Such limitations on the award do not apply where no defence has been stated or proceeded with or where there has been unreasonable conduct or a lack of good faith or in relation to an appeal to the sheriff principal[4]. Such an appeal is to lie on a point of law only[5]. Where the pursuer is neither a partnership or a body corporate nor acting in a representative capacity, he may require the sheriff clerk to effect service of the summons on his behalf[6]. There are, effectively, no rules of evidence[7]. The sheriff may remit a small claim to the summary cause or ordinary cause roll or vice versa[8].

---

1 1985 c 73. 2 1971 c 58.
3 Sheriff Courts (Scotland) Act 1971, s 35(2), (4). 4 Ibid, s 36B.
5 Ibid, s 38. 6 Ibid, s 36A. 7 Ibid, s 35(3).
8 Ibid, s 37(2B), (2C).

The Order

1.15 The Lord Advocate exercised the powers so given to him by the Small Claims (Scotland) Order 1988[1]. That Order, along with the appropriate Act of Sederunt, brought the new small claims procedure into operation on 30 November 1988. The procedure is to be used for actions for payment of money not exceeding £750 in amount (exclusive of interest and expenses), other than actions in respect of aliment and interim aliment and actions of defamation. It is also to be used for actions *ad factum praestandum* and actions for the recovery of possession of moveable property where a sum not exceeding £750 is claimed as an alternative. For these purposes, actions *ad factum praestandum* include actions for delivery and actions for implement but not for count, reckoning and payment. If the value of the claim does not exceed £200 no award of expenses may be made but in any other case a maximum of £75 may be awarded by way of expenses.

The Rules

1.16 Also brought into force on 30 November 1988 was the Act of Sederunt (Small Claim Rules) 1988[2] which, as its title suggests, contains the rules for small claims. There are no more than 41 rules but some of the ordinary cause rules and some of the summary cause rules also apply as indicated by Appendices 2 and 3 respectively. Appendix 1 provides the various forms to be used, starting with forms for the appropriate summons, which require litigants to do little more than fill in the appropriate boxes. Rule 34 provides the sheriff with the now common dispensing power to relieve parties, where appropriate, of the consequences of failure to comply with the rules.

Other provisions

1.17 Although the above Act, Order and Act of Sederunt provide the complete structure for the small claims procedure a

---

1 SI 1988/1999. 2 SI 1988/1976.

number of other provisions were brought into force on the same date which are of direct relevance to small claims. Principal among these is the Debtors (Scotland) Act 1987[1] which makes provisions for allowing the debtor extensions of time to pay and a completely new code for enforcement of decrees by diligence. Relative Forms and Rules of procedure are given in the Act of Sederunt (Proceedings in the Sheriff Court under the Debtors (Scotland) Act 1987) 1988[2]. The Sheriff Courts (Scotland) Act 1971 (Privative Jurisdiction and Summary Cause) Order 1988[3] increased both the summary cause upper limit and the privative jurisdiction of the Sheriff Court to £1,500. The Legal Aid (Scotland) Act 1986 Amendment Regulations 1988[4] excluded small claims processes at first instance from legal aid[5]. Legal aid may still be available for appeals. Finally, the Scottish Courts Administration has produced a leaflet entitled *Small Claims in the Sheriff Court* and a more detailed booklet entitled *A Guide to Small Claims Procedure in the Sheriff Court* which offer guidance in a simple form to the new small claims procedure.

---

1 1987 c 18.   2 SI 1988/2013.   3 SI 1988/1993.
4 SI 1988/2289.
5 By amending the Legal Aid (Scotland) Act 1988 (c 47), at Sch 2, Pt II, para 3.

2 PARTIES

STARTING POINT

2.01 When anyone considers making a small claim against another person, the first questions which have to be answered are – Can I sue? and – Who can I sue? At this point the law applicable to small claims procedure is the same as that applying to any other Scottish civil action. As in any other process, before a person can bring or defend a small claim, three attributes are necessary, viz, (1) capacity, (2) title and (3) interest. This chapter will first briefly discuss the question of title and interest to sue and then discuss that and the question of capacity further in relation to particular classes of litigants.

TITLE AND INTEREST TO SUE

2.02 Quite apart from having the capacity to sue, a litigant, and in particular a pursuer, must always demonstrate that he has both a title and interest to sue[1]. Both may be conveniently dealt with together since title and interest, although they are different, often very much run into each other[2]. To have a title to sue, the litigant must be a party to some legal relation which gives him some right which the person against whom he raises the action either infringes or denies[3]. It may well be that a contract entered into between A and B has the result of conferring some benefit on C, but that does not mean that C will have a title to sue for performance of the

---

1 *D & J Nicol v Dundee Harbour Trs* 1915 SC (HL) 7 at 12 per Lord Dunedin.
2 *Summerlee Iron Co. Ltd. v Lindsay* 1907 SC 1161 at 1165 per Lord Dunedin.
3 *D & J Nicol v Dundee Harbour Trs* above.

contract or for damages for defective performance. If, for example, a client instructs a solicitor to draft a will benefitting a third party and, after his death, it is discovered that, due to the negligence of the solicitor, the will does not have the effect of benefitting the third party, that would not mean that the third party would have a title to sue the solicitor[1]. The question of whether the necessary legal relation exists to give a title to sue in any particular case is, however, a question of substantive law rather than procedure. In each case reference has to be made to the authorities on the branch of law concerned.

2.03 'Interest' is a word of wide meaning. In the context of interest to sue it may be said that the litigant must have some benefit from asserting the right with which the action is concerned or from preventing its infringement. For example, where the next of kin of a deceased person raised an action to reduce his last will, which would have the effect of setting up a prior will which did not benefit the next of kin either, it was held that the next of kin had no interest to pursue the action. The action was, accordingly dismissed[2]. The interest may be small[3] or contingent[4] and is not limited to pecuniary or patrimonial interest, but may be an interest in any right recognised by law[5]. In general a party with a pecuniary interest has a title to sue[6], and probably also where he has any real interest[7].

2.04 The pursuer must have a title to sue at the date of the raising of the action[8] and a continuing title to pursue the action to final judgment[9]. The date of the raising of a small claim is, as in an ordinary action, the date of the service of the summons[10]. However, if

---

1 *Robertson v Fleming* (1861) 4 Macq 167; *Weir v J M Hodge & Son* 1990 SLT 266.
2 *Swanson v Manson* 1907 SC 426; cf. *Agnew v Laughlan* 1948 SC 656; *Graham v Graham* 1968 SLT (Notes) 42.
3 *Strang v Steuart* (1864) 2 M 1015 at 1029 per Lord Justice-Clerk Inglis.
4 *Hannah v Hannah's Trustees* 1958 SLT (Notes) 9; *Hayes v Robinson* 1984 SLT 300.
5 *Gunstone v Scottish Women's Amateur Athletic Association* 1987 SLT 611.
6 *Doherty v Norwich Union Fire Insurance Society Ltd* 1974 SC 213 at 220 per Lord Robertson.
7 *Summerlee Iron Co Ltd v Lindsay* 1907 SC 1161.
8 *Symington v Campbell* (1894) 21 R 434.; *Eagle Lodge Ltd v Keir and Cawdor Estates Ltd* 1964 SLT 13.
9 *Donaghy v Rollo* 1964 SC 278.
10 *Alston v MacDougall* (1887) 15 R 78.

the pursuer has basically a good title, which he needs to have formally completed, he may complete it during the course of the action[1]. If he has no title at all at the raising of the action, a subsequent assignation in the course of the proceedings will not help him[2] nor will an averment that the party with the true title to sue has consented to the action[3]. Where the person who first sues has no title or interest to sue or ceases to have any during the course of the action, amendment may be allowed and another pursuer whose title to sue is unchallengable may be sisted in his place to continue the action[4]. An averment that the defenders had acted in *mala fide* to deprive the pursuer of his title to sue in the course of the action was allowed to go to proof[5].

2.05 A party who wishes to defend an action must also have a title and an interest to do so. Generally, where someone has been called as a defender by the pursuer, the pursuer will not be heard to object to his title to defend[6]. There may be circumstances in which it could be held, however, that although the defender has been called, he has no interest to defend[7]. More difficult questions arise in cases where someone who has not been called to defend an action seeks to do so. In such cases, where the would-be defender can demonstrate that his legitimate and material interests would be prejudiced by the granting of decree, he may apply by Minute to enter the Process[8].

1 *Lanarkshire Health Board v Banafaa* 1987 SLT 229; *David Boswell Ltd v William Cook Engineering Ltd* 1989 SLT (Sh Ct) 61; *Doughty Shipping Co Ltd v North British Railway Co* 1909 1 SLT 267; *Donald v Nicol* (1866) 5 M 146.
2 *Symington v Campbell* (1894) 21 R 434; *Bentley v MacFarlane* 1964 SC 76, 1964 SLT 58; *Mirowave Systems (Scotland) Ltd v Electro-Physiological Instruments Ltd* 1971 SC 140); 1971 SLT (Notes) 38.
3 *Hislop v MacRitchie's Trustees* (1881) 8 R (HL) 95; *Eagle Lodge Ltd v Keir and Cawdor Estates Ltd* 1964 SLT 13.
4 *Donaghy v Rollo* 1964 SC 278; *A C Stewart & Partners v Coleman* 1989 SLT 430; but cf. *Jack v MacKay* 1990 SCLR 816.
5 *M'Dowall v M'Ghee* 1913 2 SLT 238.
6 *Murray's Trustees v St Margaret's Convent* (1906) 8 F 1109 at 1116–1117 per Lord Kinnear; *Low v Scottish Amicable Building Society* 1940 SLT 295 at 296 per Lord Patrick; *M'Lauchlan v M'Lauchlan's Trustees* 1941 SLT 43 at 44 per Lord Robertson.
7 *Schaw v Black* (1889) 16 R 336.
8 SCr 21A; see para **7.05** below and cf. *Glasgow Shipowners' Association v Clyde Navigation Trustees* (1885) 12 R 695; *Gas Power and By-Products Co Ltd v Power Gas Corporation Ltd* 1911 SC 27; *Zurich General Accident and Liability Insurance Co v Livingston* 1930 SC 582.

CLASSES OF LITIGANTS

Children

2.06 The law governing the capacity of children to sue and to be sued is now set out in the Age of Capacity (Scotland) Act 1991 (c 50). Formerly, a child under the age of 12 years in the case of a girl and 14 in the case of a boy, was described as a pupil and was said to be in pupillarity. From then until the age of 18 the child was known as a minor and was said to be in minority. A pupil had no capacity to sue or to be sued by himself. His affairs were under the control of his tutor/tutrix, who would normally be his parent(s)[1]. In some cases, however, his tutor might be a person nominated by his deceased parents[2] or a person appointed by the court[3] or even a local authority where parental rights had been taken over under the Social Work (Scotland) Act 1968[4]. A minor had capacity to raise an action or to defend one but the conduct of his affairs was supervised by his curator/curatrix, whose consent was required for the raising of an action.

2.07 The Age of Capacity (Scotland) Act 1991 has abolished this two-stage system and replaced it with a system whereby a child under the age of 16 years has no capacity to enter into any transaction[5], including the bringing or defending of, or the taking of any steps in, civil proceedings[6]. There is now a system of guardianship for children under the age of 16 years, with the law previously applicable to a tutor in relation to his pupil now applying to the guardian[7]. Curatory is abolished altogether[8]. Where the pursuer is under the age of 16 years, the action has to be raised on his behalf by his guardian, narrating in the instance that he is 'A as guardian and administrator-at-law of B[9]'. However, where an action has been raised without the guardian, it will be sufficient if the guardian later enters appearance to concur in the action[10]. Where it is sought to sue a child as defender, the action must be against the child and his guardian. If the latter is unknown

---

1 Law Reform (Parent and Child) (Scotland) Act 1986 (c 9) ss 2(1) and 8.
2 Ibid, s 4(1).   3 Ibid, s 3(1).   4 1968 c 49, ss 16 ff.
5 1991 Act, s 1(1)(a).   6 Ibid, s 9.   7 Ibid, s 5(1).
8 Ibid, s 5(3).   9 *Carrigan v Cleland* (1907) 15 SLT 543.
10 *Keith v Archer* (1836) 15 S 116 at 118.

the action must be against the child and 'his guardians, if he any has', who should be cited in terms of rule 6 of the Small Claims Rules. Failure thus to call the guardians will result in any decree being null[1]. A guardian who conducts a litigation on behalf of a child is *dominus litis* and is personally liable for the expenses if he is not successful[2]. In the absence of a guardian appearing for a child, either as pursuer or defender, or in the event of a conflict of interest, the court may appoint a curator *ad litem*[3].

2.08 Where a child under 16 years of age does litigate without his guardian, but no exception is taken to that, and the litigation is resolved in favour of the child, it is good against the other party[4]. Where no appearance is entered for a child defender, but he has been properly cited, along with his guardians, if he has any, the decree in absence granted against him in an ordinary action will be good but subject to reponing in the future[5]. Reponing is not, of course, open in a small claim and it is difficult to see that the period of time allowed for recall of the decree by rule 27(2) could be extended. In order to avoid such problems arising as well as to safeguard the interests of any child litigant the court will, in most cases, appoint a curator *ad litem* to any child litigant appearing without a guardian[6] or where the guardian has an adverse interest[7], and that on the motion of either party or *ex proprio motu* on becoming apprised of the party's nonage[8]. Such appointment may not be made, however, where it does not appear that the guardian is not acting in the best interests of the child by refusing to concur[9] or that his concurrence has simply not been sought[10]. The curator

---

1 *Earl of Craven v Lord Elibank's Trustees* (1854) 16 D 861; *Thomson v Livingston* (1863) 2 M 114.
2 *White v Steel* (1894) 21 R 649; *Wilkinson v Kinneil Cannel and Coking Coal Co Ltd* (1897) 24 R 1001.
3 See para **2.08** below.
4 1991 Act, s 1(3)(f)(i); *Sinclair v Stark* (1828) 6 S 336 at 338.
5 *Sinclair v Stark; Dick v M'Ilwham* (1828) 6 S 798.
6 1991 Act, s 1(3)(f)(ii); *Kirk v Scottish Gas Board* 1968 SC 328; *M'Conochie v Binnie* (1847) 9 D 791; *Drummond's Trustees v Peel's Trustees* 1929 SC 484; *Cunningham v Smith* (1880) 7 R 424.
7 *Bogie v Bogie* (1840) 3 D 309; *Brianchon v Occidental Petroleum (Caledonia) Ltd* 1990 SLT 332.
8 *Drummond's Trustees v Peel's Trustees* 1929 SC 484 at 493 per Lord President Clyde. *M'Dowall v Carson* (1908) 24 Sh Ct Rep 72; *Rankine* (1821) 1 S 51.
9 *Kirk v Scottish Gas Board* 1968 SC 328 at 331 per Lord Guthrie.
10 *Carrigan v Cleland* (1907) 15 SLT 543.

ad litem, on appointment, becomes the *dominus litis*, with, for example, power, in the exercise of his discretion, to compromise the action[1].

Insane persons

2.09   From the leading case of *Moodie v Dempster*[2] it is clear that a person who is insane has no *persona standi in judicio* and, therefore cannot appear in his own name either as pursuer or defender, nor is the proper procedure to appoint a curator *ad litem* in the course of an action[3]. A petition should be presented to the court for appointment of a curator *bonis*, at whose instance the action may proceed. If a pursuer becomes *incapax* after the action has been raised, time must be given for the presentation of such a petition. Where it is proposed to raise an action against an insane person to whom a curator *bonis* has already been appointed, the action should be against the curator[4]. A person who is mentally ill is not necessarily, for these purposes, insane[5], and, in cases of doubt a preliminary proof may be allowed[6]. In the context of a small claim, however, any such question would probably best be canvassed at the hearing, though it might be possible to resolve the matter at the preliminary hearing if facts (eg the terms of psychiatric reports) were sufficiently admitted.

Trustees, executors, etc.

2.10   Among persons handling the affairs of others in a fiduciary capacity are trustees, executors, judicial factors and, mentioned above, curators *bonis* and curators *ad litem*. Actions raised by or against such persons should give their individual names in the instance together with an explanation of the capacity in which they sue or are sued. eg 'AB [designed], CD [designed] and EF [designed] the surviving trustees [or executors or whatever] acting

---

1 *Dewar v Dewar's Trustees* (1906) 14 SLT 238.   2 1931 SC 553.
3 *McGaughey v Livingstone* 1991 SCLR 412.
4 *Latta, Noter* 1977 SLT 127.
5 *Gibson v Gibson* 1970 SLT (Notes) 60.
6 *AB v CB* 1937 SC 408.

under the trust-disposition and settlement of the late GH [designed]' or 'AB [designed] the judicial factor on the estate of the firm of CD and Sons [designed] in terms of the decree of [Court and Date]'. 'The trustees of AB' or 'the representatives of the late X' without more will not do[1]. As long as the actual trustees are named it will not matter if it turns out that some of those named are not actually trustees[2]. Decree will not be granted against the non-trustees, who should be deleted from the instance by amendment. The action may be raised where the pursuers have basically a good title to sue, although something more may be required to complete the title before decree, such as a judicial factor obtaining extract of his appointment[3], or executors obtaining confirmation[4] or even an assignee of such executors having his title completed by their obtaining confirmation[5]. Where there are a number of trustees there must be a majority insisting in the action or defence[6]. A beneficiary is not entitled to sue for a debt due to the estate, but if the executor refuses to raise an action, the court may allow the beneficiary to sue in the executor's name[7]. Where a proposed defender is dead and there is no trustee or executor, the action should be raised for decree *cognitionis causa tantum*, calling as defenders all the known next-of-kin of the deceased[8]. Where he dies during the course of the action, the action may be transferred against such representatives[9].

Individual traders

2.11 Businesses carried on under a business name by a single individual are sometimes erroneously referred to as 'one-man

1 *Bell v Trotter's Trustees* (1841) 3 D 380; *Kay v Morrison's Representatives* 1984 SLT 175.
2 *Trustees for the Religious Community of Poor Clares Colettines, Edinburgh v Burns* 1939 SLT (Sh Ct) 2.
3 *Calver v Howard, Baker & Co* (1894) 22 R 1.
4 *Chalmer's Trustees v Watson* (1860) 22 D 1060; *Bones v Morrison* (1866) 5 M 240; *Symington v Campbell* (1894) 21 R 434 at 437 per Lord Adam.
5 *Mackay v Mackay* 1914 SC 200.
6 *Graham v Graham* 1968 SLT (Notes) 42; *Campbell v Campbell's Trustees* 1957 SLT (Sh Ct) 53.
7 *Morrison v Morrison's Executrix* 1912 SC 892.
8 *Smith v Tasker* 1955 SLT 347.; *Stevens v Thomson* 1971 SLT 136 at 137 per Lord Fraser.
9 *Davidson, Pirie & Co v Dhile's Representatives* (1900) 2 F 640; cf para **7.04** below.

partnerships'. Such a business is not a partnership. The firm has no separate *persona* from the individual and the rules of jurisdiction applicable, for example, are those relating to individuals and not those relating to firms. However, any person carrying on a business under a trading or descriptive name may sue or be sued in such trading or descriptive name alone[1]. He may of course, sue or be sued in his own name and it is quite common, and arguably best, to specify his own name with the business name added, as eg 'John Smith [designed] trading as [or "carrying on business under the name of"] Bagpipes and Blues Record Shop'. If he fails to state his name and an address at which service will be effective, in legible characters, on all business letters and other documents, in terms of section 4 of the Business Names Act 1985[2], he risks having any action brought by him to enforce a contractual right dismissed in terms of section 5.

Multiple pursuers

2.12 It can happen that two or more individuals wish to take action to recover small claims together. If the aggregate of the claims falls within the financial limits of the small claims procedure, then that procedure must be adopted[3]. The general rule, however, is that parties cannot accumulate their actions in one libel, except where (1) there is some connection between the parties in the matter pursued for – meaning some title or interest in common – or (2) the parties suing are aggrieved by the same act[4]. The ground of action by each pursuer must be identical and there must be no material prejudice to the defender by the pursuers' combining in one action[5], and, of course, each pursuer must separately state what his claim is. This situation most clearly arises in cases of delict, where, for example, a number of people are injured in a road accident[6] or by a single slanderous statement[7].

---

1 OC, r 5.7.   2 Act 1985, c 7.
3 *Sloan v Mycock* 1992 SLT (Sh Ct) 23 was a small claim which seems to have had two pursuers and eight defenders.
4 *Paxton v Brown* 1908 SC 406; *Feuars of Orkney v Stewart of Burray* (1741) Mor 11986; *Brims & Mackay v Patullo* 1907 SC 1106; *Boulting v Elias* 1990 SLT 596.
5 *Buchan v Thomson* 1976 SLT 42 at 44 per Lord Fraser.
6 *Buchan v Thomson* above.
7 *Harkes v Mowat* (1862) 24 D 701; *Mitchell v Grierson* (1894) 21 R 367.

The matter is more difficult in cases of contract, combined actions being incompetent unless the claims of the pursuers are interconnected[1]. In *Arbuckle v Kennedy*[2] the sheriff allowed four pursuers, each with a separate contract but in identical terms and entered into simultaneously, to sue together for identical claims, but in view of the ruling in *Boulting v Elias*[3] that each pursuer must demonstrate that he has a title to enforce the contract of the other or has an interest to do so, that was probably going too far. Where a claim, as laid, is incompetent because of a multiplicity of unconnected pursuers, however, the court will allow amendment to delete one or more and allow matters to proceed in respect of one (or, presumably, more if competent)[4]. Having separate small claims might increase the total amount of expenses recoverable from the defender[5].

Multiple defenders

2.13 In general, a claim against two or more defenders on separate grounds, inferring separate liability will be dismissed as incompetent[6]. However, where the defenders are liable jointly, or jointly and severally for the same claim, whether by agreement[7] or from the nature of the claim[8], they may be sued in one claim[9]. Joint and several liability means that each defender is liable to the pursuer for the whole of the claim, so that the pursuer is entitled to look to any one of them for payment, though, as between themselves, the defenders are liable *pro rata*, each for his own proportionate share. Therefore, if the debt has already been constituted or is expressed in writing the pursuer may sue any one defender, leaving him to seek relief against the others, but, otherwise, the pursuer must call all the defenders within the jurisdiction of the

---

1 *Feld British Agencies Ltd v James Pringle Ltd* 1961 SLT 123, at 126 per Lord President Clyde; *Killin v Weir* (1905) 7 F 526; *Fishof v Cheapside Bonding Company Ltd* 1972 SLT (Notes) 7.
2 1985 SLT (Sh Ct) 17.   3 1990 SLT 596.
4 *Paxton v Brown* above; *Boulting v Elias* above.
5 See para **9.09** below.   6 *Hook v McCallum* (1905) 7 F. 528.
7 *Western Bank v Douglas* (1860) 22 D 447; *Croskery v Gilmour's Trustees* (1890) 17 R 697; *Richmond v Grahame* (1847) 9 D 633.
8 *Grunwald v Hughes* 1965 SLT 209.   9 See Note 3 on p 21.

court[1]. Where defenders are liable only jointly, however, each is liable to the pursuer only for his share of the claim. Accordingly, where a pursuer does sue two or more defenders (they should be designated 'First' and 'Second', etc) he should state that the claim is against them 'jointly and severally', otherwise joint liability only may be presumed. Where liability is joint and several, of course, the pursuer may be paid only once, so that recovery against one defender satisfies the claim and action cannot be taken against another[2]. However, the test is satisfaction and not merely the obtaining of a decree which remains unpaid and may be worthless[3]. No transaction between the pursuer and one of the co-defenders can prejudice the right of any defender found liable to the pursuer to seek relief from the co-defender, so that the pursuer may abandon against one defender but continue to pursue against another[4].

Partnerships

2.14 A partnership has a separate *persona* distinct from its several partners. As such, it may sue or be sued in its own name with or without the addition of the names of the individual partners[5]. In any event, a partnership carrying on a business under a trading or descriptive name may sue or be sued in that name alone, in terms of Ordinary Cause rule 5.7. Any partner or partners may raise an action or defend in the name of the firm, but if there is a dispute, the majority view prevails. So, if a majority of the partners disclaim an action raised or a defence stated in the name of the firm, the action may be dismissed or the defences repelled[6].

2.15 There are, in fact, three ways to frame the instance. If, for example, three partners, AB, CD and EF, carry on business in the

---

1 *Neilson v Wilson* (1890) 17 R 608.   2 *Balfour v Baird & Sons* 1959 SC 64.
3 *Steven v Broady Norman & Co* 1928 SC 351; *Arrow Chemicals Ltd v Guild* 1978 SLT 206; *Hamilton Leasing Ltd v Clark* 1974 SLT (Sh Ct) 95; *Royal Bank of Scotland v McKerracher* 1968 SLT (Sh Ct) 77.
4 *Hardy v British Airways Board* 1983 SLT 45; *Singer v Gray Tool Co (Europe) Ltd* 1984 SLT 149.
5 *Forsyth v John Hare & Co* (1834) 13 S 42. Partners not so named are not 'defenders' – Cf *A & E Russell Ltd v General Maintenance International* 1993 SLT (Sh Ct) 83.
6 *Hutcheon and Partners v Hutcheon* 1979 SLT (Sh Ct) 61.

name 'AB & Associates', the firm may be named alone – 'AB & Associates, carrying on business at [address]' – or the partners may be sued as carrying on that business – '(First) AB [designed], (Second) CD [designed], and (Third) EF [designed] carrying on business under the style of AB & Associates'[1] – or the firm may be sued with the addition of the partners – '(First) AB & Associates, a partnership carrying on a business at [address] and (Second) AB [designed], (Third) CD [designed] and (Fourth) EF [designed] as partners thereof and as individuals'. It is suggested that, in making a claim against a partnership, the latter course is preferable as it is best to make clear that the firm is being sued but the identity of the partners should also be established. A decree against a firm is enforceable against any of the partners thereof, but it avoids dispute as to whether the person, against whom it is sought to enforce it, is or was a partner, if he is brought into the action in the first place.

2.16 The Business Names Act 1985 applies to a partnership carrying on a business under a name which does not consist of the surnames or corporate names of all the partners with no additions[2]. Accordingly, if the firm fails to state in legible characters on all letters and other business documents the name of each partner and an address at which service may be effected, in terms of section 4, there is a danger of a claim made by the firm being dismissed in terms of section 5.

2.17 While a partnership has a legal personality of its own, it does not survive independently of the partners. If they agree to dissolve or if one partner dies, the firm dies with them, even if a new set of partners carries on under the old firm name[3]. The surviving partner or partners have title to sue in their own name[4] and an action raised in the wrong name may be amended to show them as pursuers[5]. The style would be 'AB [designed] and CD [designed] the whole surviving partners of the now dissolved firm of AB & Associates, which carried on business at [address] as such

---

1 *Plotzker v Lucas* 1907 SC 315.   2 1985 c 7, s 1(1)(a).
3 *Brims & MacKay v Patullo* 1907 SC 1106; *Wilson v Cook* 1954 SLT (Sh Ct) 17; *D Forbes Smith & Johnston v Kaye* 1975 SLT (Sh Ct) 33.
4 *Nicoll v Reid* (1877) 5 R 137.
5 *Wilson v Cook* above; *Anderson v Balnagown Estates Co* 1939 SC 168.

partners and as individuals.' A pursuer claiming against the former partners of a dissolved partnership should call all the surviving partners as defenders[1]. The above is, of course, subject to the
right of the partners to provide for assignation of the rights and
liabilities of the partnership upon dissolution.

Unincorporated associations

2.18 Unincorporated associations include voluntary bodies such
as social or sporting clubs, dissenting churches or charitable
organisations. Unlike partnerships, they have no legal personality
separate from their members and, except where they fall within
the terms of Ordinary Cause rule 5.7, they cannot sue or be sued in
their own name. The names of all the individual members may be
given, but it is normal to sue in the name of the office-bearers[2]. If
the constitution of the association provides how it may sue or be
sued, than that procedure should be followed[3]. If the association
can be described as 'persons carrying on a business under a trading
or descriptive name', Ordinary Cause rule 5.7 will apply and the
association may sue or be sued in that name alone[4]. A claim against
such an association may be served at any place where the business
is carried on, with preference for a place within the sheriffdom.
The decree then granted is a valid warrant for diligence against
such persons, but there may be problems if an attempt is made to
enforce the decree against someone who has not been specifically
called as a defender[5]. As ever, the good rule for pursuers is to think
at the beginning about how the claim can be enforced in the end
and to frame the instance accordingly.

2.19 Trade unions, employers' associations and friendly societies are forms of unincorporated association with particular rules.
The latter are registered under the Friendly Societies Act 1974
(c 46), section 103 of which provides rules as to legal proceedings.

1 *M'Naught v Milligan* (1885) 13 R 366; *Neilson v Wilson* (1890) 17 R 608; *Jones Sewing
  Machine Co Ltd v Smart* 1987 GWD 5-162.
2 Cf. *Lomond Roads Cycling Club v Dumbarton County Council* 1967 SLT (Sh Ct) 35.
3 *Whitecraigs Golf Club v Ker* 1923 SLT (Sh Ct) 23.
4 *Borland v Lochwinnoch Golf Club* 1986 SLT (Sh Ct) 13.
5 *Aitchison v M'Donald* 1911 SC 174.

Trade unions and employers' associations are governed by the Trade Union and Labour Relations Act 1974 (c 52). Except where a trade union is a special register body[1] it is not and must not be treated as if it were a body corporate but it is capable of suing or being sued in its own name[2]. An employers' association, on the other hand, may be either a body corporate or an unincorporated association, but where it is unincorporated it may also sue or be sued in its own name[3].

Corporate bodies

2.20   A body corporate has a legal personality and an existence entirely independent of its members. It must sue and must be sued in its own name. The most common corporations are companies incorporated under the Companies Acts, but others may be incorporated under a particular statute or by their own charter. The mode of incorporation should be stated in the instance, eg, 'AB & Co Ltd, a company incorporated under the Companies Acts and having a place of business (or having its registered office) at . . .[4]'; 'The University of Aberdeen, incorporated by the Universities (Scotland) Act 1858, section 1[5]'; 'The Glasgow Magdalene Institution, a charitable body founded in 1859 and incorporated by Crown Charter of Incorporation granted by the Privy Council in 1866[6]'. Local authorities[7] and building societies[8] are also corporate bodies but it is not normal to narrate their mode of incorporation.

2.21   A company may enter into a partnership with other companies or individuals, in which case the rules applicable to partnerships will apply to that business[9]. A company may also carry on a business under a name other than its own, and if it does so under a trading or descriptive name it may sue or be sued in that name

---

1 Defined in s 30(1) of the 1974 Act.   2 Ibid, s 2(1).
3 Ibid, s 3(1), (2).
4 The letters 'plc' at the end of the name instead of 'Ltd' indicate a public limited company.
5 *Lord Advocate v Aberdeen University* 1962 SLT 413.
6 Glasgow Magdalene Institution Ptrs 1964 SLT 184.
7 Local Government (Scotland) Act 1973 (c 65), s 2(2).
8 Building Societies Act 1986 (c 53), s 5.
9 See paras **2.14–2.17** above.

alone[1]. Where it does so the Business Names Act 1985 will also apply to that business[2].

2.22 Where a receiver is appointed to a company he has, in relation to such part of the property of the company as is attached by the floating charge by virtue of which he was appointed, power to bring or defend any action or other legal proceedings in the name and on behalf of the company[3]. He cannot sue in his own name[4] though it is usual to design the company as '(In Receivership)' and to give the name and designation of the receiver. In a winding-up of the company the liquidator, subject to the qualifications in the relevant provisions of the Insolvency Act 1986, has power to bring or defend any action or other legal proceeding in the name and on behalf of the company[5]. The style is usually 'AB and Co Ltd a company registered under the Companies Acts and having its registered office at [address] and CD [designed] the official liquidator thereof'. A claim made against a company in receivership should simply be made against the company but thought should be given to the prospects of recovering anything. In a winding-up by the court, when a winding-up order has been made or a provisional liquidator appointed, no action or proceeding can be proceeded with or commenced against the company except by leave of the court[6]. The court may, on the application of the liquidator, direct that the same should apply to a voluntary winding-up[7]. In the interval between the presentation of a petition for winding-up and the granting of a winding-up order, the court may also stay, sist or restrain any pending proceedings against the company[8]. In these circumstances, of course, the creditor's remedy, for what it may be worth, is to make a claim in the liquidation.

The Crown

2.23 It is possible to make a small claim against a government department and, indeed, the government may wish to pursue a

---

1 OC, r 5.7.   2 See para **2.17** above.
3 Insolvency Act 1986 (c 45), s 55 and Sch 2.
4 *Myles J Callaghan Ltd v Glasgow District Council* 1988 SLT 227; *Taylor Ptr* 1982 SLT 172; cf *McPhail v Lothian Regional Council* 1981 SLT 173.
5 1986 c 45, s 165 and 167 and Sch 4, Pt II.
6 Ibid, s 130(2).   7 Ibid, s 113.   8 Ibid, s 126(1).

small claim. Proceedings by or against the Crown, even by small claims procedure, are governed by the Crown Proceedings Act 1947[1]. 'The Crown' for these purposes means Her Majesty's Government in the United Kingdom[2]. In most cases, the representative of the Crown is the Lord Advocate, by or against whom the action is laid[3]. The style should be 'The Right Honourable AB, QC, [or "Lord A of B" if a peer] Her Majesty's Advocate as representing the Minister of Transport [or whatever Government Department][4]'. It is probably competent to sue the Crown by naming the Minister of the Department concerned, though that is not usual except for the Secretary of State for Scotland, who can sue or be sued in respect of any matter for which he has responsibility. It is sufficient to libel 'The Secretary of State for Scotland' without naming the individual holding the office[5]. There is a speciality of jurisdiction which is worth mentioning here. Since the Crown has its seat in any place in the United Kingdom[6], it is possible to make a claim in any sheriff court in Scotland. If the claim is made in an inappropriate court, however, the sheriff may simply remit to another court[7].

Bankruptcy

2.24 When a person is sequestrated the whole of his estate as at the date of sequestration vests in his trustee[8]. Any action for recovery of any debt forming part of that estate should, if necessary, be taken by the permanent trustee, who has power (with consent, where appropriate) to bring, defend or continue any legal proceedings relating to the estate of the debtor[9]. He may sue, and be sued, in his own name, narrating that he is the permanent trustee in the sequestration of the bankrupt. The bankrupt may still, himself, sue if the trustee does not, but if he does, of course, anything he recovers falls to the sequestrated estate and vests in the trustee. For that reason he would normally be required to find

---

1 10 & 11 Geo VI c 44.   2 Ibid, s 40(2).
3 Crown Suits (Scotland) Act 1875 (20 & 21 Vict c 44), s 1.
4 Cf. *Kinlochleven Road Transport Co Ltd v Lord Advocate* 1955 SLT (Sh Ct) 45.
5 Reorganisation of Offices (Scotland) Act 1939 (2 & 3 Geo VI c 20), s 1(8).
6 Civil Jurisdiction and Judgments Act 1982 (c 27), s 46.
7 SC, r 22.   8 Bankruptcy (Scotland) Act 1985 (c 66), s 31.
9 Ibid, s 39(2)(b).

caution for expenses in any action he raised[1], though that would seem to be unnecessary in a small claim. A small claim should not be made to recover a debt due by the bankrupt before the date of sequestration as that should form a claim in the sequestration. Where an action is proceeding at the date of sequestration, the trustee may sist himself in place of the bankrupt.

Vexatious litigants

2.25 Vexatious litigants are as likely to be encountered in small claims procedure as anywhere else. Some might think the procedure was made for them. Where the Lord Advocate applies to the Inner House of the Court of Session and satisfies the Court that any person has habitually and persistently instituted vexatious legal proceedings without any reasonable ground for instituting such proceedings, the Court may order that no legal proceedings shall be instituted by that person without obtaining the leave of a Court of Session judge on showing that the legal proceedings are not vexatious, and that there is *prima facie* ground for such proceedings[2]. Accordingly, if such an order is in force in relation to any person, he must obtain such leave before raising even a small claim in the sheriff court.

1 *Stevenson v Midlothian District Council* 1983 SLT 433 at 463 per Lord Fraser of Tullybelton.
2 Vexatious Actions (Scotland) Act 1898 (61 & 62 Vict c 35), s 1.

3 JURISDICTION

THE SHERIFF COURT

3.01 Having ascertained that there is a claim to be made and against whom it is to be made, it has then to be decided where to make the claim. Small claims must, of course, be made in the sheriff court. The rules of jurisdiction specify the sheriff court or courts in which the claim may be made. There are 49 sheriff courts in Scotland, each dealing with the business arising in its own sheriff court district. Scotland is divided into six sheriffdoms, namely. (1) Grampian, Highland and Islands; (2) Tayside, Central and Fife; (3) Lothian and Borders; (4) Glasgow and Strathkelvin; (5) North Strathclyde and (6) South Strathclyde, Dumfries and Galloway. Each sheriffdom contains a number of sheriff court districts, with the exception of Glasgow and Strathkelvin, which has only one, but which has by far the busiest court. Each sheriffdom is presided over by one sheriff principal, while each sheriff court has one or more sheriffs. Some of the smaller courts, not providing a full week's work, share a sheriff with another court.

SUBJECT MATTER

3.02 The matters which may, or rather must, be pursued by way of small claims procedure are (1) actions for payment of money other than actions in respect of aliment and interim aliment and actions of defamation and (2) actions *ad factum praestandum* or for the recovery of possession of moveable property where there is included as an alternative a claim for payment of money. In any case the money claim must not exceed a sum presently fixed at

£750 (exclusive of interest and expenses)[1]. Actions *ad factum praestandum* include actions for delivery and actions for implement (ie for an order to carry out a certain act) but do not include actions for count, reckoning and payment[2]. Any such action is a 'civil proceeding' and, accordingly, the rules determining whether or not it may be pursued in a particular court are to be found in Schedule 8 to the Civil Jurisdiction and Judgments Act 1982[3], except for the matters excluded by Schedule 9[4]. It is not impossible that Schedule 9 could apply. It excludes, for example, admiralty causes in so far as the jurisdiction is based on arrestment *in rem* or *ad fundandam jurisdictionem* of a ship, cargo or freight. If such a cause was a claim for payment of money not exceeding the prescribed amount, it would have to be by way of the small claims procedure. However, since most of the matters excluded by Schedule 9 could never form the subject of small claims procedure anyway and the occasions when the procedure would be appropriate must be very rare indeed, the applicable rules are, for all practicable purposes, those set out in Schedule 8. It is of some importance to bear in mind that the 1982 Act was largely designed to give the force of law within the United Kingdom to the 1968 Brussels Convention on Jurisdiction and the Enforcement of Judgments in Civil and Commercial Matters, to which the United Kingdom acceded on joining the EEC. Schedule 1 of the Act sets out the text, in English, of the Convention, in terms of which jurisdiction is allocated between the Contracting States. Schedule 4, based on the Convention, applies where the courts of the United Kingdom have jurisdiction in terms of the Convention, to allocate jurisdiction between the various parts of the United Kingdom. Schedule 8 applies to Scotland only and goes further. It sets out the circumstances in which the Scottish courts may exercise jurisdiction even where the Convention does not apply. Although Schedules 4 and 8 are based upon the provisions of the Convention, there are certain differences between them. Where there are such differences Schedule 4 takes precedence over Schedule 8 and Schedule 1 takes precedence over both in cases to which the Convention applies. The Civil Jurisdiction and Judgments Act 1991 (c 12) gives effect to the Lugano Convention of 1988, which covers countries beyond the EEC and has slightly different provisions from the Brussels Convention, but

---

1 Small Claims (Scotland) Order 1988 (SI 1988/1999), art 2.
2 Ibid, art 3.   3 1982 c 27, s 20.   4 Ibid, s 21(1)(b).

the 1991 Act does not alter Schedule 8 of the 1982 Act. This chapter is in no sense an exposition of these complicated Acts, for which reference must be made to specialised works[1], but it does describe the rules which will apply to all but very exceptional small claims.

GENERAL RULE: DOMICILE

3.03 The general rule is that persons shall be sued in the courts for the place where they are domiciled.[2] This general rule is excluded where rules 3, 4, 5 and 6 of Schedule 8 of the Act apply and there may be a choice of an alternative jurisdiction where rule 2 applies. These rules are discussed in some detail below, with the exception of rule 4, which can have no application to small claims. For these purposes, a person's 'domicile' is defined by the Act, with different provisions applying to individuals and to corporations or associations and some special rules. Thus, in order to be able to sue any person in a particular sheriff court, it is necessary to establish that the person concerned is (a) domiciled within the UK, (b) domiciled in Scotland and (c) domiciled within the jurisdiction of the particular sheriff court.

Individuals

3.04 The Act starts by stating when a person is domiciled in the United Kingdom, then stating when he is domiciled in any particular part of the United Kingdom and working on down to when he is domiciled in any particular place. An individual is domiciled in the United Kingdom if and only if he is resident there and the nature and circumstances of his residence indicate that he has a substantial connection with the United Kingdom[3]. The same test applies to find whether he is domiciled in Scotland[4]. An individual is domiciled in a particular place in Scotland if he is domiciled in

---

1 Eg A E Anton *Civil Jurisdiction in Scotland* (1984) and Supplement (1986) written in association with P R Beaumont.
2 1982 Act, Sch 8, r 1.   3 Ibid, s 41(2).   4 Ibid, s 41(3).

Scotland and resident in that place[1]. There is a rebuttable presumption that the substantial connection exists where the individual has been resident in the United Kingdom (and Scotland, as the case may be) for the last three months or more[2]. An individual who is domiciled in the United Kingdom but not, in respect of the above tests, in Scotland shall nevertheless be treated as domiciled in Scotland if he is resident there and not domiciled in any other part of the United Kingdom[3]. An individual may, of course, be resident and domiciled in more than one place[4].

Corporations or associations

3.05 Unlike individuals, corporations or associations cannot 'reside' anywhere, so the 'seat' of a corporation or association is treated as its domicile[5]. 'Corporation' means a body corporate and includes a partnership subsisting under the law of Scotland and 'association' means an unincorporated body of persons[6]. There is no such thing as a 'one-man partnership' and individual traders, even trading under a business name, are still individuals, their domicile being established in terms of the rules referred to in para **3.04** above[7].

3.06 A corporation or association has its seat in the United Kingdom if and only if it was incorporated or formed under the law of a part of the United Kingdom and has its registered office or some other official address in the United Kingdom or its central management and control is exercised in the United Kingdom[8]. It has its seat in a particular part of the United Kingdom (eg Scotland) if and only if it has its seat in the United Kingdom and it has its registered office or some other official address in that part or its central management and control is exercised in that part or it has a place of business in that part[9]. It has its seat in any particular place in Scotland if and only if it has its seat in Scotland and it has its registered office or some other official address in that place or its

---

1 Ibid, s 41(4).   2 Ibid, s 41(6).   3 Ibid, s 41(5).
4 *Daniel v Foster* 1989 SLT (Sh Ct) 90.
5 1982 Act, s 42(1).   6 Ibid, s 50.
7 *Northamber Plc v Ian Benson (t/a Kyle Micros)* 1990 SCLR 140.
8 1982 Act, s 42(3).   9 Ibid, s 42(4).

central management and control is exercised there or it has a place of business there[1]. For these purposes, 'business' includes any activity carried on by a corporation or association and 'place of business' is construed accordingly, and 'official address' means any address which the corporation or association is required by law to register, notify or maintain for the purposes of receiving notices or other communications[2]. It can be seen from application of the above rules that a corporation or association may have its seat in a number of places. In particular, for example, any company incorporated in the United Kingdom will have its seat in, and be subject to the jurisdiction of any sheriff court for any place where it has a place of business.

Insurance and consumer contracts; trusts; the Crown

3.07 There are specialities in relation to insurance and consumer contracts, trusts and the Crown. In terms of the Brussels Convention, in relation to insurance matters, an insurer who is not domiciled in a contracting state but has a branch, agency or other establishment in one of the contracting states shall, in disputes arising out of the operations of the branch, agency or establishment, be deemed to be domiciled in that state[3]. Similarly, where a consumer enters into a contract (other than a contract of transport) with a party who is not domiciled in a contracting state but has a branch, agency or other establishment in one of the contracting states, that party shall, in disputes arising out of the operations of the branch, agency or establishment, be deemed to be domiciled in that state[4]. Such insurers or suppliers to consumers who are, by virtue of those provisions, deemed to be domiciled in the United Kingdom, are to be treated as domiciled in the part of the United Kingdom in which the branch, agency or establishment is situated[5]. They may be sued in the sheriff court for the place where the branch, agency or other establishment is situated[6].

3.08 A trust is domiciled in a part of the United Kingdom if and only if the system of law of that part is the system of law with which

---

1 Ibid, s 42(5). 2 Ibid, s 42(8). 3 Ibid, Sch 1, art 8.
4 Ibid, Sch 1, art 13. 5 Ibid, s 44(2). 6 Ibid, Sch 8, r 2(6).

it has its closest and most real connection[1]. Where a trust, created by the operation of a statute, or by a written instrument or created orally and evidenced in writing, is domiciled in Scotland, the trustees (or a settlor or beneficiary) may be sued in that capacity in a sheriff court of any sheriffdom in which the truster, or any of the trusters, was domiciled at the date of the coming into operation of the trust[2]. Where the trust is in the form of a marriage contract, a sheriff court of the sheriffdom in which either spouse is, or was when he died, domiciled, has jurisdiction. Where no truster or spouse is or was so domiciled or where the pursuer does not possess sufficient information to determine the appropriate sheriff court, the sheriff court at Edinburgh has jurisdiction[3]. The Crown has its seat, and therefore its domicile, in every place in the United Kingdom[4], but that may be qualified for particular purposes by Order in Council[5].

SPECIAL JURISDICTION

3.09 Rule 2 of Schedule 8 of the 1982 Act provides for a number of situations where courts may exercise a special jurisdiction over a defender as an alternative to the general rule of domicile. Where these situations arise, the pursuer has a choice as to whether to sue in the courts of the defender's domicile or in the courts having the special jurisdiction, neither having precedence over the other[6]. The general rule is, however, that defenders should be sued in the place of their domicile, and the exceptions are to be strictly construed[7].

Itinerants

3.10 A person who has no fixed residence may be sued in a court within whose jurisdiction he is personally cited[8].

---

1 Ibid, s 45(3).
2 Ibid, Sch 8, r 2(7) and s 24A of the Trusts (Scotland) Act 1921.
3 Trusts (Scotland) Act 1921, s 24A.   4 1982 Act, s 46(3).
5 Ibid, s 46(4) and (5).   6 *Bank of Scotland v Seitz* 1990, SLT 584 at 587.
7 *Davenport v Corinthian Motor Policies at Lloyds* 1991 SLT 774.
8 1982 Act, Sch 8, r 2(1).

Contract

3.11 In matters relating to a contract a person may be sued in the courts for the place of performance of the obligation in question[1]. It has been held that the words 'matters relating to a contract' are wide enough to cover more than the direct contractual obligation or even a direct breach of contract[2]. However, that would seem to be inconsistent with the view of the Inner House in *Davenport v Corinthian Motor Policies at Lloyds*[3] that the words 'in matters relating to', in rule 2(3), are virtually synonymous with the words 'in proceedings based upon[4]'. Lacking any other contractual provision, the legal implication is that a debtor is bound to tender payment to a creditor at his residence or place of business[5].

Delict and quasi-delict

3.12 In matters relating to delict or quasi-delict, the defender may be sued in the courts for the place where the harmful event occurred[6]. For these purposes, 'in matters relating to' means 'in proceedings based upon[7]'.

Branch, agency or other establishment

3.13 As regards a dispute arising out of the operations of a branch, agency or other establishment, a defender may also be sued in the courts for the place in which the branch, agency or other establishment is situated[8]. There is an implication that there is a parent body outwith the jurisdiction[9] and the primary establishment should be

---

1 Ibid, r 2(2).   2 *Engdiv Ltd v Percy Trentham Ltd* 1990 SLT 617.
3 1991 SLT 774.
4 *Strathaird Farms Ltd v GA Chattaway & Co* 1993 SLT (Sh Ct) 36.
5 *Bank of Scotland v Seitz* 1990 SLT 584; cf. *Waverley Asset Management Ltd v Saha* 1989 SLT (Sh Ct) 87; *McCarthy v Abowall (Trading) Ltd* 1992 SLT (Sh Ct) 65; *Mabon v Abbey Kitchens* 1992 SCLR 537; *Timberwise Consultants Ltd v Ross & Liddell Ltd* 1993 SCLR 972.
6 1982 Act, Sch 8, r 2(3).
7 *Davenport v Corinthian Motor Policies at Lloyds* 1991 SLT 774.
8 1982 Act, Sch 8, r 2(6).
9 *Northamber Plc v Ian Benson (t/a Kyle Micros)* 1990 SCLR 140.

of the same character as the 'other establishment[1]'. This provision is not, therefore, a backdoor method of founding jurisdiction on an individual's place of business.

Presence of property

3.14 Where the defender is not domiciled in the United Kingdom, he may be sued in the courts for any place where (a) any moveable property belonging to him has been arrested or (b) any immoveable property in which he has any beneficial interest is situated[2]. Since there is no corresponding provision in the 1968 Convention[3], this provision cannot apply in any case where the defender is domiciled in one of the contracting states. Accordingly, the court may exercise this jurisdiction only if the defender is not domiciled in the United Kingdom nor any other of the contracting states.

Multiple defenders

3.15 Where there are a number of defenders, they may all be sued in the courts for the place where any one of them is domiciled[4].

CONSUMER CONTRACTS

3.16 Rule 3 of Schedule 8 makes special provision for consumer contracts, as there defined. These provisions are based on Articles 13, 14 and 15 of the 1968 Convention[5] but there are some differences. Rule 3 will not apply, so far as it is different from the Convention, in any case in which the defender is domiciled in a contracting state other than the United Kingdom. A consumer contract first of all presupposes a 'consumer' who must have

---

1 *Courtaulds Clothing Brands Ltd v Knowles* 1989 SLT (Sh Ct) 84.
2 1982 Act, Sch 8, r 2(8).   3 Ibid, Sch 1.
4 Ibid, Sch 8, r 2(15)(a).   5 Cf ibid, Sch 1.

concluded the contract for a purpose which can be regarded as being outside his trade or profession[1]. The contract must be (a) a contract for the sale of goods on instalment credit terms, or (b) a contract for a loan repayable by instalments, or for any other form of credit, made to finance the sale of goods, or (c) any other contract for the supply of goods or a contract for the supply of services if, either the consumer took in Scotland the steps necessary for the conclusion of the contract or the proceedings are brought in Scotland by virtue of section 10(3)[2]. Section 10(3) applies to proceedings covered by the 1968 Convention and, basically, presupposes a situation where the consumer is domiciled in Scotland while the defender is domiciled in a contracting state other than the United Kingdom. In such a situation the requirement of the Convention, so far as part (c) above is concerned, is that in the state of the consumer's domicile the conclusion of the contract was preceded by a specific invitation addressed to him or by advertising and that the consumer took in that state the steps necessary for the conclusion of the contract[3]. Article 14 then allows the consumer to bring proceedings against the other party in the the courts of the contracting state in which he himself is domiciled. Section 10(3) then provides that any proceedings so brought in the United Kingdom shall be brought in the courts of the part of the United Kingdom in which the consumer is domiciled. Accordingly, if a domiciled Scotsman, in response to advertising in England enters into a consumer contract in England with a firm domiciled in Germany, he may still bring an action in the Scottish courts. For the purposes of rule 3 consumer contracts do not include contracts of transport or contracts of insurance[4].

3.17 Where the rule applies to a consumer contract as described above the consumer has a choice of court in which he may bring proceedings against the other party. He may sue the other party either in the courts for the place where the other party is domiciled, or in the courts where he himself is domiciled or in any court having jurisdiction by virtue of rule 2(6) (branch, agency or establishment,

---

1 Ibid, Sch 8, r 3(1).
2 Ibid, r 3(1); cf *Waverley Asset Management Ltd v Saha* 1989 SLT (Sh Ct) 87; *Lynch & Co v Bradley* 1992 SCLR 373, 1993 SLT (Sh Ct) 2; *Chris Hart (Business Sales) Ltd v Niven* 1992 SCLR 534; but cf *Clydesdale Bank Plc v Ions* 1993 SCLR 964.
3 1982 Act, Sch 1, art 13(3).   4 1982 Act, Sch 8, r 3(2).

cf para **3.13** above)[1]. Proceedings may be brought against the consumer by the other party, on the other hand, only in the courts for the place where the consumer is domiciled[2]. The provisions of the rule may be departed from only by an agreement entered into after the dispute has arisen or which allows the consumer to bring proceedings in a court other than a court indicated by the rule[3].

PROROGATION OF JURISDICTION

3.18 If parties have agreed that a court is to have jurisdiction to settle any disputes which have arisen or which may arise in connection with a particular legal relationship, that court has exclusive jurisdiction[4]. This rule does not apply to consumer contracts (see para **3.17** above). Rule 5(1) follows the terms of the Convention[5], but the fact that the word 'exclusive' has been omitted from the corresponding provisions of Schedule 4, art 17, has given rise to a view that, as between different parts of the United Kingdom, it is not possible to agree that the courts of one part shall have exclusive, as opposed to concurrent, jurisdiction[6]. If this view were correct it would mean that parties could agree to any court having exclusive jurisdiction except one in another part of the United Kingdom, which seems hardly correct[7]. A more recent case has held that it is possible to prorogate jurisdiction exclusively to another part of the United Kingdom[8]. The effect of the omission would seem to be that, if there is jurisdiction in the Scottish courts, an agreement to prorogate the jurisdiction of a court elsewhere in the United Kingdom will not exclude the jurisdiction of the Scottish courts unless the prorogation is specifically stated to be exclusive[9]. Any such agreement conferring jurisdiction must be

---

1 1982 Act, Sch 8, r 3(3).
2 1982 Act, Sch 8, r 3(4); *Lynch & Co v Bradley; Chris Hart (Business Sales)] Ltd v Niven* above; references in rule 3 to rule 2(9) are irrelevant to small claims procedure.
3 1982 Act, Sch 8, r 3(6).
4 1982 Act, Sch 8, r 5(1).   5 1982 Act, Sch 1, art 17.
6 *British Steel Corporation v Allivane International Ltd* 1989 SLT (Sh Ct) 57; 1988 SCLR 562.
7 See criticism of the above case in the commentary to the SCLR report and at 1989 SLT (News) 364.
8 *Jenic Properties Ltd v Andy Thornton Architectural Antiques* 1992 SLT (Sh Ct) 5.
9 *McCarthy v Abowall (Trading) Ltd* 1992 SLT (Sh Ct) 65.

either in writing or evidenced in writing or, in trade or commerce, in a form which accords with practices in that trade or commerce of which the parties are or ought to have been aware[1]. Any court on which a trust instrument has conferred jurisdiction has exclusive jurisdiction in any proceedings brought against a settlor, trustee or beneficiary, if relations between these persons, or their rights or obligations under the trust are involved[2]. Where the agreement or the trust instrument confers jurisdiction on the courts of the United Kingdom or of Scotland, without being more specific, the proceedings may be brought in any court in Scotland[3]. A defender may also prorogate the jurisdiction of a court simply by entering appearance, except where he does so solely to contest jurisdiction[4]. In a small claim it would be sufficient to appear at the preliminary hearing and raise the question of jurisdiction. If that plea was then rejected or if it proved necessary to proceed to a hearing on the issue of jurisdiction, a defence might then be stated.

AVERMENTS OF JURISDICTION

3.19 There is no requirement, as in ordinary causes, to make specific averments as to the ground of jurisdiction[5]. Nevertheless, the court has a duty to take note where there is no apparent jurisdiction compatible with the 1982 Act, even where the defender does not enter appearance[6]. Accordingly, where the ground of jurisdiction is not readily inferred, eg from an individual being designed in the instance as resident within the jurisdiction, a clear statement of what it is should be made. Summary cause rule 22, which applies to small claims, gives the sheriff wide powers to transfer a cause to any other court if he considers it expedient to do so, which he would do if it appeared that the claim should have been made in another sheriff court which would have jurisdiction[7].

---

1 1982 Act, Sch 8, r 5(2).   2 Ibid, r 5(3).
3 Ibid, r 5(4).
4 Ibid, r 6; *Clydesdale Bank Plc v Ions* 1993 SCLR 964.
5 OC r 3.1(5).   6 rr 10(4), 13(2); 1982 Act, Sch 8, r 8.
7 *Wilson v Hay* 1977 SLT (Sh Ct) 52.

4 MAKING THE CLAIM

THE SUMMONS

4.01 Small claims are initiated by a summons in a form as prescribed by the Small Claim Rules[1]. Blank forms may be obtained from the nearest sheriff court and may be sought by calling there, by telephone or by post. The sheriff clerk's staff will offer help and advice on procedure, such as which form should be used and the correct way to fill it in, but cannot give legal advice on the merits of the claim. There are, in fact, three different forms which may be used, depending on the remedy sought. The remedies which may be sought by way of small claim are:

'(a) actions for payment of money not exceeding £750 in amount (exclusive of interest and expenses), other than actions in respect of aliment and interim aliment and actions of defamation;
 (b) actions *ad factum praestandum* and actions for the recovery of possession of moveable property where in any such action *ad factum praestandum* or for recovery there is included, as an alternative to the claim, a claim for payment of a sum not exceeding £750 (exclusive of interest and expenses)[2].'

For these purposes, actions *ad factum praestandum* include actions for delivery and actions for implement but do not include actions for count reckoning and payment[3]. Where the claim is for payment of money only, Form 1 should be used. Where the claim is for delivery or for the recovery of possession of moveable property, with the alternative of payment, Form 15 is appropriate. Where the claim is for implement of an obligation, with the alternative of payment, Form 18 should be used. In addition to the above cases, an ordinary action or a summary cause, which could have been a

---

1 Act of Sederunt (Small Claim Rules) 1988 (SI 1988/1976).
2 Small Claims (Scotland) Order 1988 (SI 1988/1999), art 2.
3 Ibid, art 3.

41

small claim but for the financial limit, may be treated as a small claim if the parties so agree[1].

Form 1

4.02 Form 1 must be used when making a claim for payment of money only[2]. The first page has six boxes which require to be filled in. After the pursuer has filled in the other boxes, box 5 and the smaller box at the top right of the page are completed by the sheriff court staff. The name, address and telephone number of the sheriff court in which it is intended to make the claim must be entered in box 1. This may well but need not be the court which supplied the form. Figure 1 shows a page completed by the pursuer, including box 1. The name and address of the pursuer is entered into box 2 and the name and address of the defender in box 3, as also shown in Figure 1. These latter two boxes form together what is known as 'the Instance', setting out who are the parties to the action. Where the parties sue in some special capacity[3] that should be made clear. The reference, in box 3 in Figure 1, to the defender's 'residing at' the address in the Instance, may be accepted, where not challenged, as sufficient indication that the defender is domiciled within the jurisdiction[4]. There is space to enter, in box 4, the sum of money claimed and any interest which is to be claimed on it. The sum must, of course, be no more than £750. The rate of interest normally awarded is presently 8%[5], but, if there is justification for it, a higher rate may be sought[6]. Interest runs automatically from the date of decree but if it is sought from an earlier date it must be specifically claimed, except in damages claims[7]. Form 1 seeks it from the date of service, but it could be a different date. If the pursuer is being represented by a solicitor, that solicitor's name, full address and telephone number must be entered in box 6[8]. If the pursuer has no solicitor, box 6 should be left blank.

1 Sheriff Courts (Scotland) Act 1971 (c 58), s 37(2C).
2 r 3(1).   3 See Chapter 2 above.   4 Cf para **4.06** below.
5 Act of Sederunt (Interest in Sheriff Court Decrees or Extracts) 1993, SI 1993/769.
6 *Bank of Scotland v Davis* 1982 SLT 20.
7 Interest on Damages (Scotland) Act 1971 (c 31); *Orr v Metcalfe* 1973 SC 57.
8 SC r 3A.

SMALL
CLAIM
FORM 1

Small Claim Summons

Claim for Payment of Money

OFFICIAL USE ONLY
SUMMONS No.
RETURN DATE
PRELIMINARY HEARING DATE

1 Sheriff Court (name, address and tel. no.)

GLASGOW SHERIFF COURT
1 CARLTON PLACE
GLASGOW G5 9DA   Tel no: 041-429 8888

2 Name and address of person making the claim. (PURSUER)

HENRY BROWN
12c GLEBE STREET
GLASGOW

3 Name and address of person from whom money is claimed (DEFENDER)

ISABELLA BLACK or WHITE
residing at 12a GLEBE STREET
GLASGOW

4 CLAIM

The Pursuer claims from the Defender the sum of £ **300.00** _____ with interest on that sum at the rate of **15** % annually from the date of service and expenses.

5

RETURN DATE		19	
PRELIMINARY HEARING DATE		19	at am

* Sheriff Clerk to delete as appropriate

The Pursuer is authorised to serve* form 2/form 3, which is a service copy summons, on the defender not less than 21 days before the RETURN DATE shown in the box above. The summons is warrant for arrestment on the dependence.

Sheriff Clerk Depute .... Date .... 19.....

Name, full address and tel. no. of pursuer's solicitor (if any)

6

NOTE:
The person making the claim (the pursuer) should complete boxes 1,2,3,4 and 6 on this page and the statement of claim on page 2 and the Sheriff Clerk will complete box 5 when he receives this form from the pursuer.

1

Figure 1

Arrestment on the dependence/to found jurisdiction

4.03   The warrant to serve which is signed by the sheriff clerk, in box 5, contains a warrant to arrest on the dependence[1]. Arrestment is a procedure whereby a creditor who seeks payment from a recalcitrant debtor, and who knows of moveable property belonging to the debtor in the hands of a third party, may prevent the third party from giving it back or parting with it in any way. The creditor may further require the third party to make the property available to him in payment or part payment of the debt by an ordinary action of furthcoming. Arrestment can thus be a valuable protection for a creditor, and a pursuer in a small claim may obtain similar protection for the payment of his claim by arrestment on the dependence of the action. Summary cause rules 47 and 48 apply to the small claims procedure and rule 47 refers to arrestment to found jurisdiction as well as on the dependence. However, the occasions when arrestment to found jurisdiction would have much relevance to a small claim must be very few indeed[2]. If it were ever appropriate, warrant to arrest to found jurisdiction may be sought to be added to the warrant in box 5[1].

4.04   The warrant to arrest is sufficient for execution anywhere in Scotland[3] and must be executed by a sheriff officer, who must have the warrant with him when he does so. The rules governing such execution are as for any ordinary action and need not be detailed here[4]. The arrestment falls unless the summons is served within 42 days from the date of execution of the arrestment. The pursuer or his solicitor must report the execution of service forthwith to the sheriff clerk, the certificate of execution being on the same paper as the summons[5]. The defender may have the arrestment on the dependence loosed on paying into court, or finding caution to the satisfaction of the sheriff clerk in respect of, the sum claimed plus £50 expenses[6]. The sheriff clerk issues a certificate which operates as a warrant for the release of the arrested property and sends a copy of it to the person who instructed the arrestment[7]. The

---

1 r 3(6).   2 Cf paras **3.02** and **3.14** above.
3 SC r 11.
4 Reference may be made, eg to Sheriff I D Macphail's *Sheriff Court Practice*, Chap 11.
5 SC r 47; *Cluny Investments Services Ltd v MacAndrew & Jenkins, WS* 1992 SCLR 478.
6 SC r 48(1).   7 r 48(2).

defender may also apply to the sheriff, by minute intimated to the pursuer, to recall or restrict the arrestment, with or without consignation[1]. Where the application is granted the sheriff clerk grants a certificate which is warrant for release of the arrested property to the extent ordered by the sheriff[2].

The statement of claim

4.05   On page 2 of Form 1, the first box is for the statement of claim. In this box the pursuer must enter a statement of the facts which are said to justify the claim so as to give fair notice to the defender[3]. It is not necessary, at this stage, to set out any legal proposition which is to be founded upon. Figure 2 shows an example. The statement must include details of the basis of the claim including relevant dates[4]. Where the claim arises from the supply of goods or services, a description of the goods or services and the date or dates on or between which they were supplied and, where relevant, ordered must be given[5]. Mail order firms and similar businesses, which keep running accounts, sometimes do not retain full details of transactions and seek to rely on computerised accounts. It has been held that a claim on that basis, which does not give the details required by the rules, is incompetent[6], at least in relation to the similar rules for summary causes. On the other hand, it has also been said that the courts should adopt a liberal and enabling approach in small claims procedure and not require such details where they are of no practical importance[7]. The apparent view that the approach should be sufficiently liberal and enabling as to ignore the plain requirements of the rules does not, however, have universal support and, in particular, in *North of Scotland Hydro-Electric Board v Braeside Builders' Trustees*[8], Sheriff Principal R C Hay commented:

---

1 SC r 48(3).   2 SC r 48(4).   3 r 3(4).
4 r 3(4)(a).   5 r 3(4)(b).
6 *GUS Catalogue Order Ltd v Oxborrow* 1988 SLT (Sh Ct) 2; but cf *Littlewoods Warehouses v Adam* 1988 SLT (Sh Ct) 4.
7 *British Gas plc v Darling* 1990 SLT (Sh Ct) 53.
8 1990 SLT (Sh Ct) 84.

STATE CLAIM HERE OR ATTACH A STATEMENT OF CLAIM—(to be completed by the pursuer)

1. The defender has refused or delayed to pay the sum claimed.

2. The details of the claim are* THE DEFENDER IS DOMICILED IN GLASGOW
THE PURSUER AND DEFENDER LIVE IN NEIGHBOURING FLATS REACHED THROUGH
A COMMON CLOSE AND STAIR AT 12 GLEBE STREET. THERE ARE 4 OTHER FLATS.
FOR SOME TIME THE CLOSE HAS BEEN IN A DELAPIDATED STATE REQUIRING TO BE
REPAINTED. THE PURSUER APPROACHED THE OCCUPIERS OF THE OTHER FIVE FLATS.
ALL BUT THE DEFENDER AGREED TO THE CLOSE BEING REPAINTED. THE PURSUER
ENGAGED A PAINTER WHO DID THE NECESSARY WORK FOR A PRICE OF £1,800.
THE PURSUER PAID THE PAINTER AND COLLECTED 1/6 th (£300) FROM
EACH OF THE OCCUPIERS EXCEPT THE DEFENDER WHO REFUSED TO PAY

*If necessary attach a separate sheet. HER 1/6 th SHARE.

Figure 2

'While I support in principle the proposition that the courts should be prepared to adopt a liberal and enabling approach in the small claims procedure, I respectfully dissent from the proposition that this approach should be universally applied. In my opinion, different considerations may apply where a party is represented by skilled advisers and where a party is an unrepresented party litigant. I do not consider that a liberal and enabling approach should be universally adopted so as to excuse insufficient identification of the disputed issues by solicitors or other skilled advisers. Nor do I consider that the fact that any particular pursuer has a large volume of claims should be an excuse for error'.

4.06 The statement of claim must also contain a reference to any agreement which the pursuer has reason to believe may exist giving jurisdiction over the subject matter of the small claim to another court[1] and a reference to any proceedings which the pursuer has reason to believe may be pending before another court involving the same cause of action and between the same parties as those named in the summons[2]. Figure 2 shows a statement of the ground of jurisdiction. This is not strictly necessary, but it is certainly preferable, particularly if a ground other than domicile is founded on. In any event, the sheriff will not grant decree unless it is clear from the terms of the summons that a ground of jurisdiction does exist[3], so there must be some indication of the ground of

---

1 r 3(4)(c).   **2** r 3(4)(d).   **3** rr 10(4), 13(2).

jurisdiction somewhere in the summons. The box provided on the form may not be large enough to accommodate the full statement of claim, in which case, as indicated on the form, it may be set out on a separate piece of paper and attached.

THE BOOK OF SMALL CLAIMS

4.07 The completed Form 1 must be taken or sent to the sheriff court in which the claim is being made. The pursuer must, at this stage, pay a fee to the sheriff clerk, which is presently £6 for a claim for less than £50 of money, and £32 for any other claim[1]. The sheriff clerk inserts in box 5 the return date, which is the last date on which the defender must return a response form to the sheriff clerk[2]. Immediately beneath that he must insert the date for the preliminary hearing, which is seven days after the return date[3]. The return date is calculated with reference to the period of notice which must be given to the defender[4]. The sheriff clerk keeps a Book of Small Claims in terms of rule 28 and he gives the new summons an appropriate number of the entry of the case in the Book, which is entered in the box at the top right of the summons along with the return date and the preliminary hearing date. The sheriff clerk enters in the Book of Small Claims a note of all small claims, minutes for recall of decree under rule 27 or for variation of decree in terms of summary cause rule 92. At this first stage the sheriff clerk will enter the names, designations and addresses of the parties, the nature of the cause, the amount of the claim, the date of issue of the summons and the return date. As the case proceeds he enters further details as appropriate in terms of the rule. The Book may be made up of separate rolls, each relating solely to proceedings of a particular description of small claim. The Book, which is open for inspection during normal business hours, is signed in respect of each court day by the sheriff.

---

1 Sheriff Courts Fees Order 1985 (SI 1985/827), as amended by SI 1993/2957.
2 r 4(5).
3 r 12(2) and (3).
4 See para **4.08** below.

SERVICE ON THE DEFENDER

Period of notice

4.08   The summons is then signed by the sheriff clerk, although he must refer it to the sheriff for signing if the defender's address is unknown or if, for any other reason, he is not happy about signing it[1]. Service must be made on the defender before the commencement of the period of notice prior to the return date. That period is 21 days where the defender is resident or has a place of business within Europe or 42 days where he is resident or has a place of business outwith Europe[2]. If the address of the defender is unknown, the sheriff fixes the period of notice[3]. Where service is by post, the period of notice starts from the beginning of the day next following the date of posting[4]. It is provided that, where the period of notice expires on a Saturday, Sunday, public or local holiday, the period of notice shall be deemed to expire on the first following day on which the sheriff clerk's office is open for business[5]. Those who drafted the rules must have had little confidence in sheriff clerks if they thought that such dates might be fixed as return dates. Where service is not properly effected in time, warrant for re-service may be sought from the court and a new return date will be given[6]. As in any other action, the date of commencement of the small claim will be the date of service upon the defender[7].

Form 2 or 3: time to pay direction

4.09   The form of the summons which is to be served on the defender (known as 'the service copy summons') is either Form 2 or Form 3. Form 2 is served in cases where the defender is entitled to apply for a time to pay direction[8] and Form 3 where he may not[9]. Time to pay directions may be applied for in terms of the Debtors (Scotland) Act 1987 (c 18). A time to pay direction is an order by

---

1 r 3(5).	**2** r 4(1), (2).	**3** r 6(1).
4 r 4(4).	**5** r 4(3).	**6** SC r 12.
7 *Alston v MacDougall* (1887) 15 R 78.		**8** r 3(2).
9 r 3(3).		

which the court directs that any sum awarded by the court shall be paid by specified regular instalments or as a lump sum at the end of a specified period and may be made by the court on application by the debtor[1]. The debtor must be an individual[2]. The few other restrictions on a time to pay direction, which might be relevant to small claims, are that it is not competent where the sum sued for is in respect of rates or taxes[3] or where a time order under section 129(2)(a) of the Consumer Credit Act 1974, for the payment by instalments of the same sum, has previously been made[4]. In connection with the latter point, if the claim is by a creditor or owner seeking to enforce a regulated agreement within the meaning of the Consumer Credit Act 1974, the pursuer must lodge a copy of any existing or previous time order relating to the debt[5]. Accordingly, in most cases, where the defender is an individual, or a guardian, judicial factor or curator *bonis* for an individual, Form 2 should be served and in all other cases, Form 3. Prior to service, the pursuer must complete Section A, which is on page 4 of Form 2 and page 3 of Form 3. This ensures that the case is identified when the defender returns these pages to the sheriff clerk.

Where the defender has a known address in Scotland

4.10 Service may be effected on a defender whose address in Scotland is known either by post or by a sheriff officer. The warrant on the summons is sufficient authority for service anywhere within Scotland[6]. Postal service is done by a solicitor, a sheriff officer or the sheriff clerk sending the service copy summons by first class recorded delivery post[7]. On the face of the envelope there must be printed or written a notice in Form 5[8]. This ensures that, if the letter cannot be delivered, it is returned to the sheriff clerk as evidence of failure to serve. Service can also be made by a sheriff officer tendering the service copy summons to the defender personally or by leaving it in the hands of an inmate at the defender's dwelling place or an employee at the defender's

---

1 Debtors (Scotland) Act 1987, s 1.
2 Ibid, s 14(1).   3 Ibid, s 1(5).   4 Ibid, s 14(3).
5 Act of Sederunt (Proceedings under the Debtors (Scotland) Act 1987) 1988 (SI 1988/2013, r 7(1).
6 SC r 11.   7 r 5(1).   8 r 5(5).

place of business[1]. If the sheriff officer has tried but been unsuccessful in serving the summons in any of those ways, he may, after making diligent enquiries, serve the summons either by depositing it in the defender's dwelling place or place of business by means of a letter box or other lawful means or by affixing it to the door of the defender's dwelling place or place of business[2]. In either case he must thereafter also send a letter containing a copy of the summons by ordinary post to the address at which he thinks it most likely that the defender may be found[2]. It is to be noted that the requirement for the sheriff officer to be accompanied by a witness does not apply to small claims procedure[3]. In all cases there must be enclosed with the service copy summons a form of service in Form 4 of the small claim rules[4]. There must not be included in the same envelope as the service copy summons any document not forming part of the summons or any form of response or other notice in accordance with the rules[5]. This is intended to prevent pursuers including their own 'advice' to the defender as to payment with expenses to avoid decree, and the like, which seems to be given a spurious authority by inclusion in the envelope and might serve to confuse defenders.

4.11 Although citation by sheriff officer is always an option, postal service should normally be tried first. It is cheaper and easier and, even where the defender does not respond, the court might not allow the cost of citation by sheriff officer as part of the expenses awarded, unless postal citation was first tried and failed or a good explanation is given for not attempting it. Where the pursuer is not a partnership or a body corporate or acting in a representative capacity he may require the sheriff clerk to effect service on his behalf[6], in which case he may also require the sheriff clerk to supply him with a copy of the summons[7]. Such service will usually be postal but if it is to be by sheriff officer, the pursuer must first pay the prescribed fee (presently £21) to the sheriff clerk[8]. After service has been effected, by whatever manner, a certificate of service in Form 6 (signed by the person effecting it),

---

1 SC r 6(1) and (4).   2 SC r 6(2).
3 SC r 6(3), omitted from Appendix 3 to Small Claims rules.
4 r 5(4).   5 r 32.
6 Sheriff Courts (Scotland) Act 1971 (c 58), s 36A.
7 r 5(2).
8 r 5(3): Sheriff Court Fees Order 1985 (SI 1985/827) as amended by SI 1993/2957.

describing the manner in which service was effected, must be attached to the summons[1]. Blank forms are printed on page 3 of the Principal Summons supplied by the court. Again, the envelope must contain no unofficial document[2].

Where the defender's address is outwith Scotland

4.12 Where the defender's address is outwith Scotland different rules apply[3]. Service may be made on a defender at a known residence or place of business in England and Wales, Northern Ireland, the Isle of Man, the Channel Islands or any country with which the United Kingdom does not have a convention providing for service of writs in that country either in accordance with the rules for personal service under the domestic law of the place where service is to be effected or by posting the service copy summons in Scotland in a registered or recorded delivery letter, or the nearest equivalent which the postal services permit, addressed to the defender at his residence or place of business[4]. If the citation is by personal service in accordance with the domestic law of such a country, other than the United Kingdom, the Channel Islands or the Isle of Man, the pursuer must lodge a certificate, by a person who is conversant with the law of the country concerned and who practises or has practised as an advocate or solicitor in that country, or who is a duly accredited representative of the government of that country, stating that the form of service employed is in accordance with the law of the place where the service was effected[5].

4.13 Service may be effected on a defender in a country which is a party to the Hague Convention on the Service Abroad of Judicial and Extra-Judicial Documents in Civil or Commercial Matters dated 15 November 1965 or the European Convention on Jurisdiction and Enforcement of Judgments in Civil and Commercial Matters as set out in Schedule 1 to the Civil Jurisdiction and Judgments Act 1982 (The Brussels Convention) in one of five ways[6]. Firstly, it may be by a method prescribed by the internal

---

1 r 5(6).   2 r 32; cf. para **4.10**, above.
3 r 5(7).   4 SC r 9(1)(a).   5 SC r 9(6).
6 SC r 9(1)(b).

law of the country where service is to be effected for the service of documents in domestic actions upon persons who are within its territory[1]. In such a case, a certificate as described at the end of para **4.12** above must be lodged[2]. Secondly, service may be effected by or through a central authority in the country where service is to be effected at the request of the Foreign Office[3] or, thirdly, by or through a British Consular authority at the request of the Foreign Office[4]. In either of these two cases the pursuer must (a) send a copy of the summons and warrant for service with citation attached with a request for service to be effected by the method indicated in the request to the Secretary of State for Foreign and Commonwealth Affairs and, (b) lodge in process a certificate of execution of service signed by the authority which has effected service[5]. Fourthly, where the law of the country in which the defender resides permits, by posting in Scotland the service copy summons in a registered or recorded delivery letter or the nearest equivalent which the available postal services permit, addressed to the defender at his residence[6]. Fifthly, where the law of the country in which service is to be effected permits, service may be made by an *huissier*, other judicial officer or competent official of the country where service is to be made[7]. In such a case, the pursuer, his solicitor or a sheriff officer must (a) send to the official in the country in which service is to be effected the service copy summons and warrant for service, with citation attached, with a request for service to be effected by delivery to the defender or his residence and (b) lodge in process a certificate of execution of service by the official who has executed service[8]. It is provided by summary cause rule 18(8) that in the case of a defender domiciled in another part of the United Kingdom or in another contracting state (to the Brussels Convention) the sheriff shall not grant decree in absence until it has been shown that the defender has been able to receive the summons in sufficient time to arrange for his defence or that all necessary steps have been taken to that end. Further, summary cause rule 18A provides that where the summons has been served in a country which is party to the Hague Convention decree shall not be granted until it is established to the satisfaction of the sheriff that the requirements of article 15 of that Convention

---

1 SC r 9(1)(b)(i).   2 SC r 9(6).   3 SC r 9(1)(b)(ii).
4 SC r 9(1)(b)(iii). 5 SC r 9(4).   6 SC r 9(1)(b)(iv).
7 SC r 9(1)(b)(v).   8 SC r 9(5).

have been complied with. Article 15, inter alia, also requires it to be established that service was effected, in an appropriate manner, 'in sufficient time to enable the defendant to defend'. It is not at all clear what tests the sheriff has to apply[1]. Clearly, however, sheriff clerks should not simply grant decree in absence in such cases but should bring them specifically to the attention of the sheriff.

4.14 Postal service on a defender outwith Scotland in terms of the above provisions must be by a solicitor, sheriff officer or the sheriff clerk and the forms for citation, the certificate of citation and the notice on the face of the envelope apply as for postal service in Scotland[2]. Whatever the form of service, every summons, citation and notice on the face of the envelope must be accompanied by a translation in an official language of the country in which service is to be effected, unless English is an official language of that country[3], and the translation must be certified as a correct translation by the person making it[4]. The certificate must contain the full name, address and qualifications of the person making it and must be lodged along with the certificate of execution of citation. While an individual pursuer may require the sheriff clerk to effect service for him on a defender outwith Scotland in any of the above ways[5], the sheriff clerk will not instruct such service until payment of the cost of it has been made to him by the pursuer[6].

Where the defender's address is unknown

4.15 Where the pursuer does not know the defender's address the summons must be put to the sheriff, who may, if satisfied that the court has jurisdiction over the defender, grant warrant to serve the summons either by the publication of an advertisement in Form 7 in a newspaper circulating in the area of the defender's last known address or by displaying on the walls of court a copy of a notice in Form 8[7]. In either case the sheriff fixes the period of notice[7]. It is better, for the avoidance of doubt, to specify the

---

1 Reference should be made to Anton *Civil Jurisdiction in Scotland*, paras **7.31–7.36**.
2 SC r 9(3) and (4); cf paras **4.10** and **4.11** above, noting r 32.
3 SC r 9(7).   4 SC r 9(8).
5 Sheriff Courts (Scotland) Act 1971 (c 58), s 36A.   6 r 5(8).
7 r 6(1).

newspaper in the warrant. The pursuer must lodge a service copy of the summons with the sheriff clerk, from whom the defender may uplift it[1], in the unlikely event of either form of publication coming to his attention. An individual pursuer may require the sheriff clerk to effect service for him in either manner[2], but only on payment by the pursuer to the sheriff clerk of the cost of doing so, in which case the pursuer may require the sheriff clerk to supply him with a copy of the summons[3]. Except where the sheriff clerk does so effect service, the pursuer must lodge a copy of the newspaper containing the advertisement[4], or a copy of Form 8, duly completed for display[5] as the case may require. If the defender's address becomes known at a later stage, the sheriff may allow the summons to be amended to show the address and, if appropriate, may grant warrant for re-service subject to such conditions as he thinks fit[6].

Return of the summons

4.16 Where service is successfully effected, other than by the sheriff clerk, the pursuer must return the summons with a certificate of service to the sheriff clerk on or before the return date, failing which the sheriff may dismiss the small claim[7]. Except where jurisdiction has been constituted by arrestment to found jurisdiction a party who subsequently appears or is represented may not object to the regularity of the service and the appearance shall be deemed to remedy any defect in the service[8].

FORMS 15 AND 18

4.17 Part III of the Small Claims Rules contains special rules for claims for delivery or recovery of possession of moveable property and for implementation of an obligation. The rules for small claims for payment of money only do apply to these other claims but only

---

1 r 6(2).   2 Sheriff Courts (Scotland) Act 1971 (c 58), s 36A.

3 r 6(3).   4 r 6(4).   5 r 6(5).

6 r 6(6).   7 r 7(1).   8 SC r 13.

in so far as they are not inconsistent with the special rules[1]. Form 15 must be used to make a claim for delivery or recovery of possession of moveable property[2], and Form 18 to make a claim for implement of an obligation[3]. The first page of these forms is noticeably different from Form 1 in that there is no space for a return date. No return date is fixed in these cases. Instead, only a preliminary hearing is fixed and set down in the summons[4]. Box 4 is also different. The claim is in four parts. The first, in Form 15, claims that 'in the circumstances set out in [the] statement of claim on page 2, [the pursuer] is entitled to possession of the article mentioned in the statement of claim'. The second asks the court 'to order the defender to deliver that article to the pursuer'. In Form 18, the first part is a claim that 'in the circumstances set out in [the] statement of claim on page 2, the defender is required to perform the duty mentioned in that statement of claim'. The second part asks the court 'to order the defender to perform that duty'. Obviously, the statement of claim on page 2 must clearly identify such articles and duties. In particular, the court will not grant an order for implement unless the alleged duty is set out in terms which will leave the defender in no doubt what it is he has to do[5]. The same considerations apply to the alternative claim for payment of money as apply in relation to Form 1[6].

4.18 Service must be made so as to give the requisite period of notice prior to the preliminary hearing. The period of notice and the methods of citation are as for Form 1 summonses. Where the summons is in Form 15, the service copy summons must be in Form 16 where the defender may apply for a time to pay direction and in Form 17 where he may not[7]. Where the summons is in Form 18, the appropriate forms for the service copy summons are Form 19 and Form 20 respectively[8]. Where service is effected other than by the sheriff clerk, the pursuer must return the summons, together with a certificate of service in Form 6, to the sheriff clerk at least 24 hours before the date of the preliminary hearing, failing which the sheriff may dismiss the claim[9].

---

1 r 35.   2 r 36(1).
3 r 37(1).   4 r 40(1).
5 Cf. *Middleton v Leslie* (1892) 19 R 801; *McArthur v Lawson* (1877) 4 R 1134; *Munro v Balnagowan Estates Co Ltd, Liqr* 1949 SC 49.
6 Cf. para **4.02** above.   7 r 36; cf para **4.09** above.
8 r 37; cf para **4.09** above.   9 r 38.

COMPUTER GENERATED FORMS

4.19   The sheriffs principal have agreed with Scottish Courts
Administration that computer generated small claims and
summary cause forms may be accepted from businesses processing
large numbers of claims. Guidelines have been issued by SCA as to
acceptable forms, which must be submitted for approval to SCA
(in hard copy or disk) by the firm which must have approval for its
use of the forms. The substitute forms must be accurate facsi-
miles of the official original, including the notes for completion of
the form, they must provide the same information as that on the
official original and must be readily recognisable as small claims/
summary causes. The official crest is not reproduced but they
must carry an agreed notation to vouch their authenticity. Details
of acceptable colour, paper size and quality, content and layout
and manner of assembly are given in the guidelines available from
Scottish Courts Administration.

5 THE DEFENDER'S RESPONSE

THE SERVICE COPY SUMMONS

5.01 The formal intimation to the defender that a small claim is being made is service of the service copy summons, which will be in Form 2 or 3[1] or Form 16 or 17 or 19 or 20[2]. Which form has been served will be evident from the top left hand corner of the first page. The differences which might apply to Forms 16, 17, 19 or 20 will be mentioned later in this chapter, which will deal with the possible responses to Form 2. The second page of Form 3 advises the defender of three possible responses, which are all possible responses to Form 2. In addition, the defender who receives Form 2 is advised of two other possible responses, since service of Form 2 indicates that a Time to Pay Direction may be applied for.

FAILURE TO RESPOND

5.02 The first possibility, in any case, is for the defender to do nothing. The defender who decides to adopt this course will have decided (a) that he has no defence to the claim, (b) that he is not able to pay in full and so avoid the decree being taken against him, and (c) that he is not entitled or able to offer proposals for payment which might form the basis of a time to pay direction. Where the defender does not respond the case is not called in court. The sheriff clerk notes the failure to respond in the Book of Small Claims[3] and if he served the summons he advises the pursuer of the failure to respond by sending him a copy of Form 10 by first class delivery post[4].

---

1 Cf. para **4.09** above.   2 Cf. para **4.18** above.   3 r 28(1)(h).
4 r 7(2).

What the pursuer should do

5.03   A pursuer who has received Form 10, and who wishes to take decree, may complete box 1 on that form and return it to the court before noon on the day prior to the preliminary hearing date. Alternatively he, and any other pursuer wishing to take decree, may return a separate minute, in Form 12, to the court before the same time or may, before then, attend at the court and enter a similar minute in the Book of Small Claims. Any of these steps may also be taken by the pursuer's solicitor or the solicitor's authorised clerk. The court may then grant decree on the date for the preliminary hearing[1]. If the pursuer fails to do any of the above, the court dismisses the claim[2]. If the pursuer is late in doing it, however, the sheriff has a 'dispensing' power to grant relief from the strict terms of the rules[3] and the pursuer would be entitled to a hearing to persuade the sheriff to do so[4]. The sheriff will not grant decree unless it is clear from the terms of the summons that a ground of jurisdiction exists[5]. Where the pursuer is a solicitor suing for an amount alleged to be due on a business account the sheriff should, in every case, remit the account to the auditor of court for taxation[6]. A decree granted in absence in terms of rule 10 is subject to recall in terms of rule 27[7].

5.04   It may well be, however, that the pursuer, for some reason, does not wish to take decree yet, but wishes to preserve his position. This would most likely happen where the defender had responded, not by intimation to the court, but by payment, or offer of payment to the pursuer. The pursuer may then wish to have the case continued to await the honouring of a cheque or to make further investigations or the like. The pursuer might then complete box 2 of Form 10 or minute separately, on the Book of Small Claims or by separate minute. The minute must, however,

1 r 10(1).   **2** r 10(2).   **3** r 34.
4 *Calcranes Ltd v Aberdeen Northern Transport* 1978 SLT (Sh Ct) 52; but cf *Swan v Blaikie* 1992 SCLR 405.
5 r 10(4).
6 *W & AS Bruce v Ewans* 1986 SLT (Sh Ct) 20; *Lyall & Wood v Thomson* 1993 SLT (Sh Ct) 21; but cf *Alex Morison & Co, WS v McCulloch* 1984 SLT (Sh Ct) 88.
7 r 10(3).

make clear what the pursuer wants the court to do. If it is simply 'To call please' or some other unspecific phrase, the claim may simply be dismissed[1].

PAYMENT IN FULL

5.05 The second possible response is to admit the debt and to pay the whole sum due including interest and expenses. As with the first response, this does not involve the defender sending anything to or attending at the court but it does avoid a decree passing against him. The defender will have concluded that he has no defence to the claim but that he is able to pay. He should then respond in good time before the return date by approaching the pursuer or his solicitor and offering payment. He may even be able to negotiate a lesser, compromise payment. Delay in making the payment may, however, result in decree being granted and possibly enforcement proceedings being commenced. This would be undesirable not only because the expenses which would be added to the debt would increase markedly, but because the fact that a decree has been granted against the defender is within public knowledge and may well affect, for example, his ability to obtain credit in the future. The pursuer who has been satisfied by payment will probably do nothing, in which case the claim will be dismissed in terms of rule 10(2), although it is possible to minute for dismissal in any of the ways mentioned in para **5.04** above. A wise defender would check with the court to ensure that decree is not being sought, whether through inadvertance or otherwise.

TIME TO PAY DIRECTIONS

Application

5.06 Defenders who are entitled to make an application for a time to pay direction should have been served with Form 2 (or 16

---

1 *Jenners Princes Street Edinburgh Ltd v McPherson* 1992 SLT (Sh Ct) 18.

SHERIFF COURT
(Including address)

Summons No _____

Return Date _____

SECTION A

Preliminary

This section must be completed
before service

Hearing Date _____

COURT STAMP
(OFFICIAL USE ONLY)

PURSUER'S FULL NAME AND ADDRESS

DEFENDER'S FULL NAME AND ADDRESS

SECTION B

APPLICATION IN WRITING FOR A TIME TO PAY DIRECTION
UNDER THE DEBTORS (SCOTLAND) ACT 1987
(payment by instalments or deferred lump sum)

CLAIM ADMITTED—I admit the claim and make application

(1) To pay by instalments of £ *7 - 00*

(tick one box only)   each week ☑   fortnight ☐   month ☐

or

(2) To pay the sum ordered in one payment within _____ weeks/months

Signature ... *Isa White* ...

To help the Court please provide details of your financial position in the boxes below
if necessary attach a separate sheet

My outgoings are:	weekly ☑	fortnightly ☐	monthly ☐		My income is:	weekly ☑	fortnightly ☐	monthly ☐
~~Rent~~/Mortgage £ *35 (£150 per month)*					Wages/Pensions £ *100/25*			
Heating £ *7*					Social Security £			
Food £ *30*					Other			
HP £ *15*								
Other *Telephone 3*								
Insurance 7								
Motor car 15 (Tax, insurance, repairs)								
Total £ *112*					Total £ *125*			

Dependants: Children—how many *0*

Dependent relatives—how many *0*

Here list all capital (if any) for example value of house; amount in bank/building society account, shares or other investments:
House £35,000 (after mortgage deducted)
Bank £500

APPLICATION FOR RECALL OR RESTRICTION OF AN ARRESTMENT

I seek the recall or restriction of the arrestment of which the details are as follows:—

Signature ....

Figure 3

or 19)[1]. It is not open to defenders who are not so entitled, and who will, therefore, have been served with Form 3 (or 17 or 20), to make such an application. Their service copy summons will not mention the two possible responses by which such an application may be made. A time to pay direction is an order by which the court directs that any sum awarded by the court shall be paid by specified regular instalments or as a lump sum at the end of a specified period and may be made by the court on application by the debtor[2]. The two responses by which the defender may apply for a time to pay direction are by (a) signing box 1 on page 3 of the service copy summons and completing section B on page 4[3] or (b) signing box 2 and, in either case, returning them to the court on or before the return date[4]. The information in section B is intended to help the court decide whether the proposals for payment are reasonable. The information should, therefore, be full and clear. Figure 3 gives an example as if the defender for Figures 1 and 2 admitted the claim and wished to ask to pay at £7 per week, without having to come to court to do so. The sheriff clerk enters the response in the Book of Small Claims and, if the summons was served by him, if the response was (a) above he sends to the pursuer by first class delivery post a copy of Form 9 or, if the response was (b), a copy of Form 11[5].

Acceptance by the pursuer

5.07 The defender who chooses the first of these options states that he does not intend to attend the court. If the pursuer decides that the defender's proposals for payment are acceptable he may, before noon on the day prior to the preliminary hearing, intimate that he does not object to the application by signing and returning to the court box 1 at the bottom of Form 9, or a minute in Form 12 or entering a minute in the Book of Small Claims[6]. Presumably, the pursuer's solicitor of authorised solicitor's clerk could also do this as rule 10(1) allows them to minute for decree 'or other order'. The pursuer having so intimated that he does not object to the time

---

1 See paras **4.09** and **4.18** above.
2 Debtors (Scotland) Act 1987 (c 18), s 1.   3 r 9.
4 r 8(1)(d).   5 r 7(2).   6 r 11(1).

to pay order, the case does not call in court but the sheriff may grant decree accordingly on the date for the preliminary hearing[1].

Preliminary hearing

5.08   If the pursuer does not indicate that he accepts the defender's proposals or if the pursuer has signed and returned box 2, indicating that he intends to appear, a preliminary hearing is held[2]. Where the defender signed box 1 and returned Section B completed, the sheriff will listen to what the pursuer has to say and consider the information in Section B and grant decree, making such order on the application as he thinks appropriate[3]. He may thus grant full decree, without any time to pay direction, or decree subject to the time to pay direction sought by the defender or decree subject to a different, reasonable time to pay direction. Where the defender signed and returned box 2, he must attend or be represented at the preliminary hearing when he may make oral representations in support of his application[4]. The sheriff will then grant decree, making such order as he thinks appropriate in respect of the application. If the defender does not appear, decree may be granted against him in terms of the summons[5]. Where a time to pay direction is made, the time which is given to the defender to pay does not begin to run until the pursuer intimates to him an extract of the decree containing the direction[6].

Expenses and interest

5.09   Where the sheriff awards expenses in a small claim, he does not grant decree until the amount has been fixed[7]. The sheriff may, but need not, include the amount of the expenses in the time to pay direction, but, if he does not, it is not competent thereafter to make a time to pay direction for the expenses[8]. If the pursuer wants to recover interest due on the decree he must serve notice on the defender by recorded delivery post or personally by an officer of the court

---

1 r 11(2).   **2** r 12(1).   **3** r 12(6).
4 r 12(5).   **5** r 13(1).
6 Debtors (Scotland) Act 1987, s 1(1).   **7** rr 25(3), 26.
8 Debtors (Scotland) Act 1987, s 1(3).

not later than 14 days before the date for payment of the last instalment or, where payment in full is to be made at the end of a fixed period, not less than 14 days before the end of that period[1]. The notice must state that the pursuer is claiming interest and specify the amount of interest claimed[2]. The interest then becomes payable after the payment of the principal sum, sums paid by the defender being ascribed first to payment of the principal then to interest[3]. No doubt, in very many cases, the procedure will ensure that pursuers regard the interest on a small claim as hardly worth pursuing.

Effect on diligence

5.10 While a time to pay direction is in force it is not competent to seek to enforce payment by serving a charge for payment or by arrestment and action of furthcoming or sale, poinding and sale, an earnings arrestment or an adjudication for debt[4]. Arrestments on the dependence or in security remain in force, so far as not recalled or restricted, but proceeding to an action of furthcoming or sale is not competent[5]. The court may, on making a time to pay direction, recall or restrict such an arrestment[6]. The court may also impose conditions on the defender and may postpone granting decree to allow the defender to fulfill such conditions[7]. So, for example, the sheriff could postpone granting decree and continue the case for a few weeks to allow the defender to make payment of a proportion of the debt, perhaps by releasing some of the arrested funds to the pursuer, then recall or restrict the arrestment on the balance and grant decree for the remainder of the debt, payable by instalments. At the end of Section B there is a box for the specification of details of any arrestment in respect of which recall or restriction is sought.

---

1 Act of Sederunt (Proceedings in the Sheriff Court under the Debtors (Scotland) Act 1987) 1988 (SI 1988/2013), r 3.
2 Debtors (Scotland) Act 1987, s 1(7).
3 Ibid, s 1(8).
4 Ibid, s 2(1).
5 Ibid, s 2(2).
6 Ibid, s 2(3).
7 Ibid, s 2(4).

Variation or recall

5.11 The court which granted a decree with a time to pay direction may, on application by the pursuer or defender, (a) vary or recall the direction if it is satisfied that it is reasonable to do so and (b) recall or restrict any arrestment in respect of the debt[1], which may be subject to the fulfilment by the defender of such conditions as the court thinks fit[2]. The application would be made on a change of circumstances. The defender, for example, might apply where his circumstances had changed for the worse, perhaps by losing his job, or the pursuer might seek an increased instalment if he discovered that the defender was, in fact, better off than he had said to the court, or if he himself was in financial difficulty. The sheriff clerk has the duty of intimating any such variation to the parties, and the variation does not take effect until such intimation[3].

Lapse of time to pay direction

5.12 If the court has ordered the defender to pay by one lump sum at the end of a specified period, and any part of it remains unpaid 24 hours after the end of that period, the time to pay direction ceases to have effect[4]. If the direction was to pay in instalments it will also cease to have effect if the date for payment of one of the instalments arrives while the defender is still at least two payments in arrears[5], or if any part of the debt remains outstanding at the end of a period of three weeks immediately following the day on which the last instalment was payable[6]. A time to pay direction also ceases to have effect on the sequestration of the debtor or his granting a trust deed or entering into a composition contract with his creditors[7] or on the death of the debtor or the transmission of the obligation to pay the debt to another person during his lifetime[8].

---

1 Ibid, s 3(1).   2 Ibid, s 3(2).   3 Ibid, s 3(3).
4 Ibid, s 4(3).   5 Ibid, s 4(1).   6 Ibid, s 4(2).
7 Ibid, s 12(2).   8 Ibid, s 14(2).

DENYING THE CLAIM

5.13   The defender may seek to defend the claim in three ways. Firstly, he may dispute the jurisdiction of the court, saying that whether or not the defender has a good claim against him, he cannot seek to enforce it in the court he has chosen[1]. Secondly, he may accept the jurisdiction of the court but maintain that the pursuer has no right to make the claim against him (a defence on the merits). Thirdly, he may admit that the pursuer is entitled to make a claim against him but maintain that it is not as much as the pursuer is asking for (a defence as to quantum). In any of these cases he must complete box 3 on page 3 of the service copy summons and return it to the sheriff clerk on or before the return date[2]. The cause will then call in court for the preliminary hearing on the date for the preliminary hearing[3], when the defender must attend and state his defence to the court[4]. Prior to the date of the preliminary hearing the defender may, but need not, lodge a written note of the defence which he proposes to state at the preliminary hearing[5]. Where he chooses to do so, he must, at the same time, send a copy of it to the pursuer[6].

FORMS 16, 17, 19 AND 20

5.14   If the defender is served with either of Forms 16 or 19, he may apply for a time to pay direction and the considerations already referred to for time to pay directions in relation to Form 2 will apply. The time to pay direction will, of course, apply only to decree for the alternative claim for a sum of money and expenses. If Forms 17 or 20 are served, as in the case of Form 3, application for a time to pay direction is incompetent. Since there is no return date where the service copy summons is in any of Forms 16, 17, 19 or 20, the defender who wishes to defend must attend at the preliminary hearing which is held in all cases[7]. At the preliminary hearing the defender may state a defence or admit the claim and

---

1 See Chapter 3, 'Jurisdiction', above.   2 r 8(1).
3 r 12(1).   4 r 12(4).   5 r 8(2).
6 r 8(3).   7 r 40(1).

make a motion for a time to pay direction[1]. An alternative method of applying for a time to pay direction is to complete Section B on page 4 of the service copy summons and return it to the sheriff clerk at least seven days before the date for the preliminary hearing[2]. The sheriff will then consider making a time to pay direction in the absence of the defender. If, however, the defender does not return Section B nor appear at the preliminary hearing, decree may be granted against him[3]. In these cases, of course, the claim for payment of a sum of money is an alternative claim and the court will usually first grant decree for the principal claim, viz, for recovery of possession of moveable property or for implement of an obligation. It is only when that has not been complied with in the given time that the pursuer may lodge with the sheriff clerk an incidental application for decree in terms of the alternative crave for payment, intimating the incidental application to the defender[4]. The pursuer must appear at the hearing of such incidental application[5]. In a defended case, where it is competent to apply for a time to pay direction, the defender may make such application, written or oral, at any time before final decree is granted[6].

---

1 r 39(1)(a).   2 r 39(1)(b).   3 r 40(2).
4 r 41(1).   5 r 41(2).   6 r 39(2).

6 THE PRELIMINARY HEARING

PURPOSE OF THE PRELIMINARY HEARING

6.01 A preliminary hearing is held where the defender has inti-mated his intention to appear in terms of rule 8(1), to challenge the jurisdiction of the court, to defend the small claim, either on its merits or to dispute the amount claimed, or to make oral applica-tion for a time to pay direction or where the defender has sought a time to pay direction, in terms of rule 9, not intending to appear, but the defender does not accept the proposal[1]. The preliminary hearing is held on the date shown on the summons, which is seven days after the return date, and may be continued to such other date as the court shall consider appropriate[2]. Where the claim is for recovery of possession of moveable property or for implement of an obligation, there is no return date and a preliminary hearing is held in every case[3]. Preliminary hearings in relation to time to pay directions have been considered fully in chapter 5 and are not further dealt with here. The purpose of the hearing is for the defender to state his defence, if any, to the claim and for the sheriff to explore the facts of the dispute with the parties, to identify the issues and, if at all possible, to conclude the case there and then on the basis of the agreed facts or an agreed settlement.

FAILURE TO APPEAR

6.02 The preliminary hearing cannot, of course, proceed if one or other or both parties fail to appear, except in the case of an application for a time to pay direction. If the pursuer appears at the

---

1 r 12(1).   **2** r 12(2).   **3** r 40(1).

preliminary hearing but the defender does not, and has not stated a defence, decree may be granted in terms of the summons[1], provided that a ground of jurisdiction exists[2]. If, however, the sheriff is satisfied that the small claim is incompetent or that there is a patent defect of jurisdiction, he may dismiss the claim[3]. Where the defender does appear but the pursuer does not, and the defender has not yet stated a defence, the court must grant decree absolving the defender[4]. Where no one appears for either side, the sheriff must, unless sufficient reason appears to the contrary, dismiss the claim[5].

Special hearings: rule 23

6.03   The defender may have submitted a written note of the defence prior to the preliminary hearing[6] or the failure to appear might be at a continuation of the preliminary hearing after the defender has appeared and stated his defence. In such a case, where one of the parties does appear but the other does not, the sheriff must fix a special hearing in terms of rule 23[7] for a date at least 14 days later. Where that is done, the sheriff clerk must forthwith intimate the time, date and place of the special hearing to the party who has failed to appear, advising him of the reason for the special hearing and that decree may be granted against him if he fails to appear or be represented at the special hearing or fails to show good cause for his failure to appear at the earlier diet[8]. Where a party appearing at a special hearing fails to show good cause for his earlier non-appearance decree by default or decree of absolvitor may be granted against him[9]. Such decree may also be granted against a party who does not appear at the special hearing[10] or at any subsequent hearing[11]. It is to be noted that the effect of these rules is that there is only ever one special hearing and it is the first

---

1 rr 13(1), 40(2).   2 r 13(2).   3 r 13(4).
4 r 13(3); *Ross & Liddell Ltd v Ahmed* 1992 SCLR 528.
5 r 23(5).   6 r 8(2).
7 *K-X Rentals Ltd v Joyce* 1992 SLT (Sh Ct) 42. There is no discretion, even if a representative does appear and then withdraws.
8 r 23(2).
9 r 23(3)(b), which requires to be read in accordance with r 23(2)(c)(ii); cf. *Guaranteed Trade Co v Melvin* 1993 GWD 11-790.
10 r 23(3)(a).   11 r 23(3)(c).

party who fails to appear who gets the benefit of it. If, for example, the defender submits his written statement of defence along with his response in terms of rule 8(1) and attends at the preliminary hearing but the pursuer does not, the sheriff must fix a special hearing. If the pursuer appears at the special hearing with a sufficient explanation for his failure to attend, but the defender is absent, the sheriff may grant decree by default. Or if both parties appear and the case is continued to a full hearing at which the pursuer appears but the defender does not, again the sheriff may grant decree by default. It may seem odd that a defender is entitled to absolvitor if the pursuer fails to appear before he has stated a defence but that there must be a special hearing if he has stated a defence. The reasoning is, presumably, that, in the former situation, it is open to the pursuer to seek recall of the decree in terms of rule 27(1), but, in the latter situation, where a defence has been stated, once decree has been granted it cannot be recalled. Any injustice can be resolved, if at all, only by appeal or reduction of the decree.

CONDUCT OF THE HEARING

6.04 Any hearing, including a preliminary hearing, is conducted in public in such manner as the sheriff considers best suited to the clarification of the issue before him and must, so far as practicable, be conducted in an informal manner[1]. Informality is a common requirement of small claims procedures, but just what amounts to informality in the context of court proceedings is not clear. It has been suggested that informal justice should be:

'Unofficial (dissociated from state power), non-coercive (dependent on rhetoric rather than force), non-bureaucratic, decentralized, relatively undifferentiated, and non-professional; its substantive and procedural rules are imprecise, unwritten, democratic, flexible, *ad hoc* and particularistic[2].'

Clearly, the Scottish small claims procedure does not even approximate to that, nor does it seem likely that any court-based, judicial process ever could. Informality in that context seems to

---

1 r 19.
2 R L Abel: *The Politics of Informal Justice* (1982 New York, Academic Press).

mean a departure from normal, adversarial procedures in order to enter into an inquisitorial style discussion with the parties. Different sheriffs have different views on how far that can be taken. Most continue to wear wig and gown and very few think it appropriate to have a seated discussion round a table[1]. The rules, whether in letter or in spirit, do not require the sheriff to 'put the litigants at their ease' and have a cosy chat with them and it is not surprising that sheriffs are reluctant to do so. They are required to make judicial decisions based on the law, and the formalities of the court system have been developed to further that process. There is a danger that an overly informal approach designed to put a party litigant at his ease and to elucidate his case may be construed as partiality. In the end, any court process is necessarily formal and the best that can be said is that the small claims procedure must be less formal than most. The Sheriff Principal of North Strathclyde has sought to ensure a measure of informality by instructing that in small claims hearings the number of persons within the bar of the court should normally be restricted to those involved in the current case and solicitors are not required to wear gowns[2]. In South Strathclyde, Dumfries and Galloway, this dispensation would appear to extend even to summary cause courts as a whole[3], though gowns would appear to be required even in small claims in Lothian and Borders, however[4].

Statement of defence and disputed issues

6.05 It is the duty of the sheriff, at the preliminary hearing, to ascertain from the parties or their representatives what the disputed issues in the small claim are and to make a note of them on the summons. It is thereafter unnecessary for a party to satisfy the sheriff on any issue which is not so noted[5]. This process must begin with the defender stating his defence to the court, which is noted on the summons by the sheriff[6], although, if the defender has lodged a written note of his defence it should be sufficient simply

---

1 See 'Small Claims in the Sheriff Court in Scotland', Scottish Office Central Research Unit, 1991.
2 North Strathclyde Act of Court (Consolidation etc) 1992, r 1.22.
3 South Strathclyde, Dumfries and Galloway, Act of Court No 7 of 1982, r 1.
4 Lothian and Borders Act of Court (Consolidation etc) 1990 No 1, r 13.
5 r 13(5).   6 r 12(4).

to refer to that. It is clear that, in order to comply with rule 13(5), the sheriff should be able to ascertain what the disputed issues are from the summons and the stated defence but, if he is not, he should adopt an inquisitorial approach in order to obtain further necessary information from the parties. Nor is rule 13(5) complied with simply by referring to the defences. The rules clearly envisage a two stage process in which, after the defence has been stated, the disputed issues are noted. The matter cannot proceed to a full hearing until that has been done. It follows that skeleton defences are unacceptable and, for example, to state no more than 'debt denied', is not to state a defence[1]. Indeed, there should be no problem from pleadings being lacking in specification at proof, such as can occur in summary causes[2], as the sheriff should demand sufficient information to enable him to identify the issues with sufficient precision or to reject anything which does not amount to a defence in law[3]. However, it is still for parties or their representatives to ensure that their defence is properly stated. It has been pointed out, that the procedure is not a free for all, in a case in which a defender was not allowed to argue for a finding of contributory negligence when it had not been noted as a disputed issue[4]. For the sheriff, getting at the real issues may be less of a problem with party litigants, who are usually only too prepared to impart a wealth of information about the dispute, relevant or otherwise, than with solicitors, who may appear alone, having received instructions at second hand, with only the scantiest knowledge of the facts. That was the situation in *Hamilton v Ansah*[5], where the solicitor for the defender moved to continue the preliminary hearing because her client was abroad and she had no instructions, or, alternatively, to state a defence of 'debt denied'. The sheriff refused both motions and granted decree for the sum claimed. On appeal, the Sheriff Principal upheld the sheriff's decision. Accordingly, whatever might be accepted in relation to ordinary or summary causes, solicitors who appear in small claims cases must ensure that they are in possession of sufficient information properly to state a defence and to identify the disputed issues.

---

1 *Hamilton v Ansah* 1990 SCLR 21.
2 Cf. *McInnes v Alginate Industries Ltd* 1980 SLT (Sh Ct) 114; *Lochgorm Warehouses v Roy* 1981 SLT (Sh Ct) 45; *Roofcare Ltd v Gillies* 1984 SLT (Sh Ct) 8.
3 *Mutch v Payne* (31 August 1992, unreported), Aberdeen, Sheriff Principal Ireland.
4 Sh. Pr. Nicholson in *Kulinski v Hassell* 1992 SCLR 499, 1993 SLT (Sh Ct) 23.
5 1990 SCLR 21.

6.06 The importance of identifying and noting the disputed issues properly can be illustrated by a number of reported cases. From the report of *North of Scotland Hydro-Electric Board v Braeside Builders' Trustees*[1], it would appear that that claim got to the full hearing without the disputed issue ever having been noted, despite both parties being represented by solicitors. On appeal Sheriff Principal Hay required to take the unusual step of remitting the case back to the sheriff to allow the adjustment of the disputed issue and to hear further evidence. He commented:

'I am driven to the view that the problem giving rise to this appeal was the failure on the part of both solicitors to identify the issues properly.'

While that would certainly appear to have been the case, it is submitted that if the sheriff presiding at the preliminary hearing had properly carried out his duty under rule 13(5), to ascertain and note the disputed issues, the problem would not have arisen. The case also, however, reflects a tendency to adopt a different approach in cases where litigants are represented from that in cases where they are not. Referring to the case of *Slessor v Burnett-Stuart*[2], Sheriff Principal Hay stated:

'I respectfully agree with the proposition that where parties are legally represented the sheriff is under no obligation to explore the disputed issues at the preliminary hearing . . .'

6.07 It is respectfully submitted that Sheriff Principal Ireland had stated no such proposition in *Slessor v Burnett-Stuart* and that such a proposition is not in accordance with the small claims rules. What the Sheriff Principal said in the latter case was that the sheriff was not bound to do more than he did. The sheriff had granted decree at the preliminary hearing on the basis of an admission that the sum sued for was due. Whilst making that admission, the defender's solicitor stated that the defender wished to lodge a counter-claim. The sheriff pointed out that there was no provision for a counter-claim in a small claim but superseded extract on the decree which he granted for three months to allow the defender time to bring his own small claim and have it disposed of. Thereafter, it seems belatedly to have occurred to the defender's solicitor that, if she had sought to plead a defence of set off, she could have maintained a defence. On appeal to the sheriff

1 1990 SLT (Sh Ct) 84.   2 1990 SLT (Sh Ct) 62.

principal she submitted that the sheriff should have made sufficient enquiry himself to ascertain that there was a defence of set off. Sheriff Principal Ireland rejected that submission, stating:

'It is true that the small claim rules contemplate a more inquisitorial attitude on the part of the sheriff than is expected in other forms of procedure; but whatever further steps a sheriff may have to take when dealing with party litigants with no legal knowledge he was not in my view bound to do more than he did in this case, when the parties were represented by solicitors. When he was told that it was admitted that the sum sued for was due, without any mention of a partial defence by way of set off, he was entitled to hold that the facts were sufficiently admitted and to grant decree there and then.'

6.08 In *Mannifield v Walker*[1], the pursuer was a party litigant who presented his own case. On appeal, Sheriff Principal Nicholson found that the legal basis on which the pursuer had been claiming had not been ascertained at the proof. It is clear from his comments that that was something which the sheriff should have done at the preliminary hearing. He stated:

'Unfortunately, I think that the absence of any clear indication of the legal basis of the respondent's claim has probably led to many of the difficulties which have arisen here. I dare say that, in many instances where a small claim is presented by a lay person, there will be no difficulty in ascertaining the legal principle which is being invoked in support of it. In other cases, however, that will not be so and in that event I think that a sheriff who hears such a case must take great care to establish what, if any, legal principle is in issue.'

and later:

'As a general rule, where a small claim hearing involves a lay party litigant (and perhaps particularly where that litigant is the pursuer), I think that it will be appropriate for the sheriff to conduct that hearing as informally as possible. . . . In that event, however, two matters must in my opinion be kept firmly in mind. The first is that . . . an attempt should be made at an early stage to be absolutely clear about the legal basis on which the claim is to be determined. . . .'

6.09 *Kostric v O'Hara*[2] was another case in which there were difficulties at the full hearing and subsequent appeal because of a lack of clarity in the noting of the disputed issues. The editorial comment at the end of the SCLR report is worth repeating:

'Since the disputed issues at a preliminary hearing require to be noted by the sheriff, it is obvious that the noting can often merely be the sheriff's interpretation

---

1 1990 SCLR 369.   2 1990 SCLR 129.

of what was said to him. It is frequently difficult to focus on the exact point which the defender wishes to raise and condense it into a few words. It is obviously good practice therefore for the sheriff to read back to the defender what he has written and receive confirmation that it embodies the "disputed issues". Where the defender is represented and has lodged written defences, these should anticipate the preliminary hearing and set out the issues which are in dispute, enabling the sheriff merely to refer to them on the principal small claim'.

6.10 If, at the preliminary hearing or at any subsequent stage of the small claim, a disputed issue noted by the sheriff is the quality or condition of an object, the sheriff may inspect the object in the presence of the parties or their representatives in court or, if it is not practicable to bring the object to court, at the place where the object is located[1]. The sheriff may also, if he considers it appropriate, inspect any place material to the disputed issues in the presence of the parties or their representatives[2]. On the joint motion of the parties, if he considers it to be appropriate, the sheriff may remit to any suitable person to report on any matter of fact[3], in which case the report will be final and conclusive with respect to the matter of fact which is the subject of the remit[4]. Before such a remit may be made, however, the parties must have previously agreed the basis upon which the fees, if any, of the person to whom the remit is made, shall be met by them[5]. Parties should not be slow to resort to such a remit in an appropriate case, even if it involves expenses. In cases where the dispute involves contested facts of a technical nature, on which the sheriff cannot be expected to be an expert, the alternatives are to lead evidence at the full hearing from competing experts, which is likely to be considerably more expensive, or to lead no expert evidence at all, in which case the parties may often just as well invite the sheriff to toss a coin. After all such enquiry as is appropriate at the preliminary hearing, however, where the sheriff is satisfied that the facts are sufficiently admitted, he may decide the small claim on the merits there and then and, if appropriate, make an award of expenses[6]. Where, on the other hand, any issue of fact between the parties is still disputed, the sheriff must appoint a date for a full

---

1 r 13(7).   **2** r 13(8).   **3** r 13(9).
4 r 13(10).   **5** r 13(11).
6 r 13(6); cf. *Slessor v Burnett-Stuart* 1990 SLT (Sh Ct) 62.

hearing[1]. It is submitted that, where there is no 'issue of fact' in dispute, the matter should be resolved without appointing a date for a full hearing even though, in an appropriate case, the preliminary hearing might be continued for a fuller debate on the law. Where there is an issue of fact which requires to be resolved, however, the disputed issues noted should include any disputed issues of law.

'I have come to the conclusion that the disputed issues to be noted by the sheriff should not be confined to issues of fact in cases where the defender, for example, raises a question of law which, in an ordinary action, would amount to a plea to the relevancy. So, if a defender's position was that the facts relied on by the pursuer did not give rise to a good claim in law, this should be stated as a disputed issue and noted as such by the sheriff.'[2]

Finally, it should be noted that the sheriff may, on the motion of a party, allow amendment of the summons, statement of claim or note of defence and adjust the disputed issues at any time[3].

6.11 Applying the above to a practical example, Figure 4 shows what the sheriff might write in the event that the defender in the example of Figures 1 and 2 intimated an intention to defend and both parties appeared for themselves at the preliminary hearing. The defender stated that she should not have to pay for any of this as she lives on the ground floor and has no interest in the stairways which were decorated and she was never consulted about it. The sheriff identified as an issue the legal question of whether a ground floor proprietor has any obligation to maintain the common stairways above the ground floor. He continued the case once and ordered the parties to produce their title deeds to see what they said about it. They were silent on the matter. He then asked the defender if she did agree that the work needed to be done and that the work was done to an acceptable standard. The defender replied that she did not accept that. The sheriff enquired further for details and the pursuer's response. He then noted the defence as shown and the four disputed issues. It can be seen that the first three disputed issues are issues of fact. The fourth is an issue of law. The sheriff could visit the tenement to see the standard of work personally.

---

1 r 13(12).
2 *Kostric v O'Hara* 1990 SCLR 129 at 130 per Sheriff Principal Mowat.
3 r 15.

FOR OFFICIAL USE ONLY

Defence (to be noted by the sheriff)

The close didn't need to be painted. It had been redecorated only 4 years before and was still in reasonably good condition. The other occupiers did not agree to it being repainted. The pursuer ordered the work without consulting anybody. The others have paid reluctantly to avoid trouble with the pursuer. In any event the work was not done to a workmanlike standard. Believed that the pursuer employed his cousin, who is unemployed and has no qualifications or experience in painting and decorating, to do the work for a grossly inflated price. The walls now look hideous and are already beginning to peel in places. Further and in any event, the defender lives on the ground floor. The pursuer lives on the first floor. There are three floors. All occupiers have to use the entrance lobby. The defender never uses the stairs. She should only have to pay 1/6 th of the cost of painting the entrance lobby.

Disputed issues (to be noted by the sheriff)

1. Whether the work required to be done at all

2. Whether the work was done to an acceptable standard

3. Whether the price was reasonable

4. What proportion should the defender have to pay, bearing in mind that she occupies a ground floor flat.

2

Figure 4

7 INCIDENTAL MATTERS

INCIDENTAL APPLICATIONS

7.01 In the course of a small claim, as with any action, incidental matters require to be dealt with. The parties may decide that they want the case to be remitted to another roll, or transferred to another court. One may wish to amend the statement of claim or defences or perhaps to abandon the case, or may wish the sheriff to grant relief from the consequences of inadvertently failing to comply with the rules. In these or other circumstances one or other party may wish to make an incidental application to the court. Unless there is specific provision otherwise, any incidental application must be lodged with the sheriff clerk and two days' notice of its being heard must be given to the other party[1]. Serving intimation by first class recorded delivery post would be an acceptable method of doing so[2]. A party, other than a partnership or body corporate, or one who is acting in a representative capacity or who is represented by a solicitor, may require the sheriff clerk to make such intimation[3]. The sheriff clerk keeps a Book of Incidental Applications in Small Claims in which he enters all such incidental applications, giving the names of the parties and their representatives, if any, the reference to the entry of the case in the Book of Small Claims, the nature of the application, whether or not the parties were present at the hearing and the interlocutor issued or order made[4]. The book is signed by the sheriff on each day on which incidental applications are heard and is open for inspection during normal business hours to all concerned without fee[5]. No particular form is required for an incidental application and a

---

1 r 33(1).
2 *Chris Hart (Business Sales) Ltd v Rome* 1993 SCLR 147.
3 r 33(2).   4 r 33(3).   5 r 33(4).

simple letter would be sufficient, provided it makes clear what it is that the court is being asked to do. The practice required in the Sheriffdom of Lothian and Borders is that two copies of the incidental application must be lodged along with the principal copy. The sheriff clerk appoints a hearing of the application and notes the date and time on the backing of all copies. The application and one copy is then returned to the applicant, the sheriff clerk retaining one copy. Presumably the sheriff clerk would retain the application if he is required to make the intimation. Unless the sheriff clerk does make the intimation, the applicant must, before the time fixed for the hearing, return the application to the sheriff clerk, with evidence of notice having been duly given, which may be either a certificate by a solicitor of posting a copy by (1) ordinary first class post, or (2) recorded delivery first class post or a holograph acceptance of notice[1].

REMITS AND TRANSFERS

Remit between rolls

7.02 A case which starts out as an ordinary cause or a summary cause, other than a small claim, may be remitted to the small claims roll. This is in terms of section 37(2C) of the Sheriff Courts (Scotland) Act 1971. The case must be one which could have been brought as a small claim except for the fact that it exceeds the monetary limit applicable to a small claim and the application to remit must be on the joint motion of the parties. On such joint motion the sheriff must direct that the cause be treated as a small claim and the cause must then be treated for all purposes (including appeal) as a small claim. The initial writ or summary cause summons, as the case may be, is treated as a small claims summons and the cause is remitted to the small claim roll occurring not more than seven days after the direction or, if there is no roll within that period, to the roll first occurring thereafter[2]. On the other hand, in terms of section 37(2B), in the case of any small claim, if the parties make a joint motion that the cause be treated as a summary cause

---

1 Lothian and Borders Act of Court (Consolidation etc) 1990 No 1, r 4.
2 r 14(2).

(not being a small claim) or an ordinary action the sheriff must grant the motion and remit the small claim accordingly. Where the sheriff is of the opinion that a difficult question of law or a question of fact of exceptional complexity is involved he has a discretion, either of his own accord or on the motion of any party to the small claim to remit the case to the summary cause or ordinary court roll. The small claim is then treated for all purposes (including appeal) as a summary cause (not being a small claim) or an ordinary cause as the case may be[1]. The small claim is remitted to the summary cause roll or ordinary cause roll, as the case may be, first occurring not sooner than seven days after the date of the direction[2]. Section 37(3) provides that a decision to remit or not to remit in terms of these provisions shall not be subject to review, but that is, presumably, only in relation to an exercise of discretion. There is no discretion, for example, not to remit in the face of a joint motion to do so. A decision not to remit would be incompetent and could, arguably, be successfully appealed against[3]. The sheriff has also a common law power to remit a case from a roll where it has no right to be to one where it ought to be[4]. Thus, if a case which should have been raised as a small claim was raised as a summary cause of another kind or if an action raised in the form of a small claim was not competent in that form, the sheriff is not bound to dismiss the action[5] but may simply remit the case to the appropriate roll.

'. . . the whole tendency of modern times is not to turn an action out of court on a technicality[6].'

Transfer between courts

7.03   Summary cause rule 22 applies to small claims and provides that a cause may be transferred to any other court, whether in the same sheriffdom or not, if the sheriff considers that it is expedient that this be done and a cause so transferred shall proceed in all

---

1 Cf *Bell v McGlennan* 1992 SLT 237.   2 r 14(1).
3 *City of Glasgow District Council v McAleer* 1992 SLT (Sh Ct) 41; but cf *City of Edinburgh District Council v Robbin* 1994 SCLR 43.
4 *Borthwick v Bank of Scotland* 1985 SLT (Sh Ct) 49.
5 It is submitted that in so far as *Tennent Caledonian Breweries Ltd v Gearty* 1980 SLT (Sh Ct) 71 suggests the contrary view, it is incorrect.
6 *Paxton v Brown* (1908) 15 SLT 662 at 666 per Lord President Dunedin.

respects as if it had originally been brought in that court. This power could be used, for example, where a small claim has been made in a court which does not have jurisdiction, to transfer it to a court which does[1]. The power is quite wide enough, however, to allow a transfer for any reason of convenience and that on the motion of a party to the sheriff or of his own accord.

Death or supervening legal incapacity of a party

7.04 Another, quite different form of transfer is where a case is transferred against the representatives of a party who has died or comes under legal incapacity during the dependence of a case. In such an event, any further proceedings in the case are null and void unless the party's representatives are sisted or the action is transferred against them[2]. The representatives may themselves wish to take up the claim, in which case they may apply to be sisted as parties in the place of the *incapax*[3]. If they decline to do so, however, the other party may lodge a minute craving transfer of the claim against them[4]. The procedure must, presumably, approximate to Ordinary Cause Rules 14.3 and 15.2, probably by intimating the minute and the pleadings to the representatives, who may then appear to object at a new preliminary hearing[5].

PARTY MINUTER

7.05 It has already been noted that a person who has not been called as a defender may, in fact, have a title and interest to defend[6]. Such a person may apply by incidental application to the sheriff for leave to enter the cause as a party minuter, and to state a defence[7]. The application must specify the applicant's title and interest to enter the cause and the grounds of the defence which he proposes to state[8]. The sheriff appoints a date for hearing the application and the applicant must serve a copy of the application

---

1 *Wilson v Hay* 1977 SLT (Sh Ct) 52.
2 *Thompson v Crawford* 1979 SLT 91.
3 OC r 25.1.   4 OC r 25.2(1).   5 OC r 25.2(2).
6 See para **2.05** above.   7 SC r 21A(1).   8 SC r 21A(2).

and the order fixing the date for the hearing on the other parties to the cause[1]. If, after hearing the applicant and any other party, the sheriff is satisfied that the applicant has shown title and interest to enter the cause, he may grant the application, making such order as to expenses as he thinks fit[2]. The party minuter is then treated as a defender and the cause proceeds against him as if the hearing were a preliminary hearing[3].

AMENDMENT

7.06   The sheriff may, on the motion of a party, allow amendment of the summons, statement of claim or note of defence and adjust the disputed issues at any time[4]. The corresponding ordinary cause rule 18.2 allows amendment 'at any time before final judgment' and amendment may be allowed in terms of that rule in the course or even after the conclusion of evidence at a proof. The discretion is at least as wide for small claims, but the sheriff will require a sufficient explanation before allowing late amendment, particularly if it might cause prejudice to the other party. Amendment could be allowed to increase the sum sued for beyond the small claim limit, in which case the cause would be remitted to the appropriate roll, unless the parties agreed to its remaining as a small claim.

COUNTER-CLAIMS AND THIRD PARTIES

7.07   There is no provision in the small claims rules either for counter-claims or for third party procedure. That does not mean that a defender is deprived of either remedy, however, as a motion could be made to the sheriff to remit to an appropriate roll if justice clearly required the counter-claim or the third party to be sued in the same process[5]. It is suggested that the court will not likely grant any such motion made later than the preliminary hearing, however, since, even in conventional summary causes, counter-claims

---

1 SC r 21A(3).   2 SC r 21A(4).   3 SC r 21A(5).
4 r 15.   5 Cf para **7.02** above.

are incompetent later than seven days after the first calling[1]. In the normal case it is clearly intended that the small claim should proceed as quickly as possible, leaving the defender to sue the pursuer on his own claim or the third party in a separate process. In *Slessor v Burnett-Stuart*[2], the sheriff granted decree but superseded extract to allow the defender to bring his own small claim. Somewhat belatedly in that case, the defender's solicitor realised that it was perfectly possible to plead a defence of set-off without making a counter-claim.

REPRESENTATION

7.08   In the conduct of a small claim a party may be represented by an advocate, a solicitor or an authorised lay representative[3]. Such lay representative may in representing a party do all such things for the preparation and conduct of a small claim as may be done by an individual conducting his own claim[4]. If the sheriff finds either that the lay representative is not a suitable person to represent the party or that he is not, in fact, authorised to do so, the lay representative must cease to represent the party[5]. These provisions allow wide scope for anyone to represent a party, whether employees, friends, relatives or lay advisers such as Citizens Advice Bureaux workers. An 'authorised lay representative' is somewhat clumsily defined as 'a person to whom section 32(1) of the Solicitors (Scotland) Act 1980 (offence to prepare writs) does not apply by virtue of section 32(2)(a) of that Act[6]'. So much for making the small claims rules easy for the lay person to follow. Section 32(1), particularly by sub-paragraph (b), provides that it shall be an offence for any non-solicitor to draw or prepare any writ relating to any action or proceedings in any court. In terms of section 32(2)(a), however, that does not apply to someone who 'proves that he drew or prepared the writ or papers in question without receiving, or without expecting to receive, either directly or indirectly, any fee, gain or reward'. The definition thus seems to

---

1 *Rediffusion Ltd v McIlroy* 1986 SLT (Sh Ct) 33.   2 1990 SLT (Sh Ct) 62.
3 r 30(1).   4 r 30(2).   5 r 30(3).
6 r 1A.

be a roundabout way of saying that the authorised lay representative must not be acting for any fee, gain or reward. Citizen's Advice Bureaux workers are warned of the consequences of accepting unsolicited boxes of chocolates and the like from grateful parties. Where a rule requires something to be done by, or intimated or sent to, a party, and that party is represented by a solicitor, it is sufficient compliance with the rule if it is done by, or intimated or sent to, the solicitor acting for that party in the claim[1].

CONTINUATIONS AND SISTS

7.09   The Summary Cause rules laid down restrictions on the circumstances in which the first calling could be continued and even then allowed only one continuation[2]. The idea was doubtless to try to ensure that matters moved on quickly but, since the circumstances in which a continuation proves of value are legion, the rule is more honoured in the breach than the observance and if the sheriff is sticky about the rules parties simply move for a sist. Small claims rule 12(2) simply provides that the preliminary hearing 'may be continued to such other date as the court shall consider appropriate'. There can, therefore, be more than one continuation of the preliminary hearing and that for a short or a long period and in whatever circumstances the court thinks appropriate. The alternative to a continuation is a sist. When the court sists an action the procedure is frozen and nothing further can happen until an application is made to recall the sist. There is no specific provision for sisting a small claim and it might appear that a sist is not altogether consistent with the quick procedure intended for small claims. However, there is no specific provision for sisting a summary cause either, but it is universally done and there is no doubt that it is competent. The same must apply to small claims. The Sheriff Principal of Lothian and Borders has made specific provision for dealing with a motion to sist a summary cause and a small claim[3]. A sist is of value when parties wish to take time to negotiate a settlement or where a remit is made to a suitable person to report, in terms of rule 13(9) and it is anticipated that it will take

1 r 31.   2 SC r 18(3).
3 Lothian and Borders Act of Court (Consolidation etc) 1990 No 1, r 4(4).

some time. There must be a sist if there is a reference to the European Court[1]. There is no doubt that a continuation of a full hearing may also be granted and there may even be a sist at that point. A small claim may also come before the court for a hearing on an incidental application[2] and that hearing may also be continued or a sist granted. The application could be to discharge a full hearing already fixed if it now appears to be inconvenient, for example, because witnesses will not be available on the date or because further investigations may be necessary. Whatever the situation, however, the procedure is clearly intended to be expeditious and the sheriff is not likely to allow unnecessary delay.

RECOVERY OF DOCUMENTS

7.10 It may happen that a party wishes to obtain a document thought to be in the hands of the other party or someone else as evidence in the case. Any party may apply to the sheriff for an order for recovery of such documents, referred to in a list of documents lodged by that party, as the sheriff considers relevant to the disputed issues[3]. The order may be sought at the preliminary hearing or by way of incidental application. The discretion of the sheriff appears wide and probably is so. There are limits on the discretion of the court to order recovery of documents in ordinary causes[4] but it may well be that these limits do not apply in small claims. The informal nature of the procedure, the wide terms of rule 18 and the fact that the normal rules of evidence are excluded[5] would all suggest that they do not. Since there is no appeal until after decree has been granted[6], when any documents ordered to be recovered will have served their purpose, it does not seem likely that the matter will be tested. If the sheriff does consider the listed documents to be relevant he may issue an order requiring the person who is said to be in possession of the documents ('the haver') to produce the documents within a given time. The party seeking to recover the documents must then serve a copy of the

1 OC, r 134, see para **7.14** below.
2 See para **7.01** above.   3 r 18(1).
4 Cf. Walker & Walker on Evidence (1964) Chapter XXIII.
5 Sheriff Courts (Scotland) Act 1971 (c 58), s 35(3).   6 Ibid, s 38.

order by first class recorded delivery post on the haver together with a certificate in Form 13[1]. Where the party is not a partnership or body corporate or acting in a representative capacity and is not represented by a solicitor, the sheriff clerk effects the service, which may be by sheriff officer on payment of the prescribed fee[2]. Presumably, service by sheriff officer is always an alternative to postal service.

7.11   Form 13 is the form of the sheriff's order and is addressed to the haver, requiring him to produce to the sheriff clerk within 7 days (or such other time as the sheriff has ordered), the order itself (Form 13), with its appended certificate signed and completed and all the documents in his possession falling within the list (which will have been enclosed with the order) together with a list or inventory of the documents produced, signed by him. He may produce the documents by lodging them personally with the sheriff clerk or by posting by registered or recorded delivery to the sheriff clerk at the court. By completing and signing the certificate, he certifies that the documents which he is producing are all he has in his possession, or that he has no such documents in his possession. If he knows of any such documents in the possession of someone else, he is required to specify the documents, when and where he last saw them, and in whose hands they were.

Confidential documents

7.12   If the haver claims confidentiality for any of the documents produced he must still produce them but he must enclose them in a separate sealed packet, which shall not be opened or put in process except by the authority of the sheriff obtained on the application of the party who sought the order, after opportunity has been given to the parties and the haver to be heard[3].

LOST DOCUMENTS

7.13   It is not unknown for documents which have been lodged with the court to become lost or destroyed in the course of a case,

1 r 18(2).   2 r 18(3).   3 SC r 39.

whether it happens while they are in the custody of the court or borrowed by parties' solicitors. Where that does happen, a copy of such document, authenticated in such manner as the sheriff may require, may be substituted and shall, for the purposes of the case, including the use of diligence, be equivalent to the original[1].

REFERENCE TO THE EUROPEAN COURT

7.14 As in any other form of action, questions of European Community law may arise in the course of a small claim. Parties are entitled to have such questions decided by the Court of Justice of the European Communities in Luxembourg. This is done by a reference to the European Court by the sheriff for a preliminary ruling under Article 177 of the European Community Treaty, Article 150 of the European Atomic Energy Community Treaty or Article 41 of the European Coal and Steel Community Treaty or a ruling on the interpretation of the Conventions on Jurisdiction under Article 3 of Schedule 2 to the Civil Jurisdiction and Judgments Act 1982 depending on the nature of the question of law which arises[2]. Such reference may be made by the sheriff of his own motion or on the motion of either party[3]. Only a court

'against whose decisions there is no judicial remedy under national law'

is bound to refer the question to the European Court. Accordingly, the sheriff is entitled, but not normally bound, to make the reference but the sheriff principal, on appeal to him, would be bound to do so. Even the sheriff principal is not bound to make the reference if it is not necessary to decide the question of Community law in order to give judgment in the small claim[4]. If the sheriff decides to make a reference, he continues the case for that purpose and, within four weeks, drafts a reference in the form of a request for a preliminary ruling of the European Court as nearly as may be in Form U of the Ordinary Cause Rules[5]. On the reference being drafted, the sheriff clerk forthwith sends a copy to each of the parties, who then have four weeks to lodge with the sheriff clerk

1 SC r 26.   2 OC r 38.1.   3 OC r 38.2.
4 *CILFIT Srl v Ministry of Health* [1982] ECR 3415, [1983] 1 CMLR 472.
5 OC r 38.2(2) and 38.3(1).

and to send to each other a note of any proposed adjustments to the draft reference[1]. The sheriff must, within 14 days after the latest date for such adjustments, consider the proposed adjustments and make and sign the reference, which the sheriff clerk forthwith intimates to the parties[2]. The case is then sisted until the European Court gives its preliminary ruling, although the sheriff may recall the sist to make any *interim* order which a due regard to the interests of the parties may require[3]. A copy of the reference certified by the sheriff clerk is transmitted by the sheriff clerk to the Registrar of the European Court, unless an appeal against making of the reference is pending[4]. However, that qualification is unlikely to be of relevance, since a reference to the European Court is not a final judgment of the sheriff and, therefore, the terms of section 38 of the Sheriff Courts (Scotland) Act 1971 would seem to preclude an appeal.

ABANDONMENT

7.15 At any time prior to decree being pronounced, the pursuer may offer to abandon the small claim.[5] The advantage of abandonment in terms of rule 22 is that the court will dismiss the claim rather than grant decree of absolvitor in favour of the defender. The latter form of decree amounts to *res judicata* so that the pursuer cannot raise a subsequent action on the same facts against the defender. Decree of dismissal, however, does not, leaving open the possibility of the pursuer seeking to make the claim again. The pursuer might wish to abandon, for example, where he realises that he has a good claim but is proceeding on quite the wrong legal basis or where essential evidence is not available in time for the hearing or, perhaps, where the claim is worth more than first thought and should have been raised in another form. It is not unknown for a pursuer to abandon while the case is at avizandum after a disastrous proof. The pursuer who wishes to abandon must, however, comply with the strict terms of rule 22. Where the offer to abandon is made, the sheriff clerk assesses the sum of expenses payable by the pursuer to the defender, calculated

---

1 OC r 38.2(2) and (3).   2 OC r 38.3(4) and (5).   3 OC r 38.4.
4 OC r 38.5.   5 r 22.

on such basis as the sheriff may direct (subject to section 36B of the Sheriff Courts (Scotland) Act 1971 and rule 26)[1]. The pursuer must make payment of the assessed sum of expenses to the defender within 14 days of the assessment, whereupon the court may dismiss the claim[2]. Although the matter is not beyond doubt, it is submitted that the word 'may' does not indicate that the court has a discretion but that the pursuer has a right to dismissal on compliance with the rule[3]. If the pursuer fails to make payment of the expenses the court must grant decree of absolvitor, with the expenses, in favour of the defender[4].

DISPENSING POWER

7.16   While rules exist to be obeyed and to ensure that justice is done as quickly, cheaply, fairly and efficiently as possible, it is not in the interests of justice that good claims or good defences should fail because of technical failure to comply with the strict terms of the rules. Most civil court procedures, therefore, provide for a power in the court to relieve parties from the consequences of failure to comply with the rules in certain circumstances. This power, referred to as a 'dispensing power' is provided to the sheriff in small claims procedure by rule 34. It provides that the sheriff may relieve any party from the consequences of any failure to comply with the provisions of the rules which is shown to be due to mistake, oversight or other cause, not being wilful non-observance of the rules, on such terms and conditions as seems just by way of extension of time, lodging or amendment of papers or otherwise so as to enable the small claim to proceed as if such failure had not occurred. While the discretion allowed to the sheriff is certainly widely expressed, its limits should be noted, particularly by those who are inclined to regard it as the safety net for the incompetent solicitor. It has recently been observed by one sheriff principal that the court is increasingly being expected to grant dispensation on the flimsiest of excuses and without proper pleading, and that the dispensing power should be used only in exceptional cases where

---

1 r 22(2).   **2** r 22(3).
3 *Singer v Gray Tool Co (Europe) Ltd* 1984 SLT 149.
4 r 22(4); *McGregor v Wimpey Construction Ltd* 1991 SCLR 868.

sound reasons exist[1]. This in an appeal in which the defaulting solicitor had the temerity to suggest that the sheriff should have got him out of his difficulty by exercising the dispensing power *ex proprio motu*!

7.17 It may be that the reference to a 'dispensing power' is misleading. The sheriff does not have power to dispense with the rules and to substitute a procedural code of his own[2], or to allow something to be done which could not competently be done at the correct time[3] or to cure a nullity[4]. The rule allows the sheriff to relieve a party from the consequences of a failure to comply with the rules. Accordingly, before the rule can operate,

'there must have been a failure to comply with the provisions of the rules, and that failure must have been by a party who requires relief from the consequences of the failure[5].'

The failure must be shown to be due to mistake, oversight or other cause, not being wilful non-observance of the rules[6]. It is not enough simply to point to a failure without adequate explanation[7]. Within its limitations a party is

'seeking an exceptional indulgence by invoking the sheriff's dispensing power. In exercising that particular power the sheriff has an unqualified discretion and his having regard to the widest interests of justice between the parties can scarcely be said to be inappropriate[8].'

'The decision on whether or not to exercise the dispensing power in any particular case is a matter within the sheriff's discretion, and is not one with which an appeal court will readily interfere[9].'

7.18 Where a summons is not timeously returned (in terms of rule 7) the sheriff clerk may not simply refuse to accept it late, as

---

1 *McMillan v Webb* 1993 SLT (Sh Ct) 28 per Sheriff Principal Hay. Cf *McGregor v Wimpey Construction Ltd* 1991 SCLR 868.
2 *Gunac Ltd v Inverclyde District Council* 1982 SLT 387.
3 *Barnes (Flexible Packaging) Ltd v Okhai (Flexible Packaging) Ltd* 1978 SLT (Notes) 72; *A & E Russell Ltd v General Maintenance International* 1993 SLT (Sh Ct) 83.
4 *Cluny Investments Services Ltd v MacAndrew & Jenkins, WS* 1992 SCLR 478.
5 *Smith v Daram* 1990 SLT (Sh Ct) 94 per Sheriff Principal Ireland; approved in *Morton v N L Sperry Sun (UK) Ltd* 1993 SCLR 342, 1994 SLT 13; but see now *Grier v Wimpey Plant & Transport Ltd* 1994 GWD 9-573. See also *Chris Hart (Business Sales) Ltd v Rome* 1993 SCLR 147.
6 *Anderson v Rollo, Davidson & McFarlane* 1992 SCLR 797.
7 Cf *Slessor v Burnett-Stuart* 1990 SLT (Sh Ct) 62 per Sheriff Principal Ireland.
8 *W Jack Baillie Associates v Kennedy* 1985 SLT (Sh Ct) 52 per Sheriff Principal Caplan; and cf *McMillan v Webb* 1993 SLT (Sh Ct) 28.
9 *Alpine House Ltd v Links* 1990 SLT (Sh Ct) 87 per Sheriff Principal Hay.

the pursuer is entitled to an opportunity to persuade the sheriff to allow it to be received late[1]. It seems to be accepted that the sheriff may allow a late minute for recall of a decree (in terms of rule 27)[2], even after extract[3]. In such a case, although a party is entitled to recall of the decree as of right where the minute for recall is timeously lodged, the allowance of the late minute being a matter for the discretion of the sheriff he may have to be persuaded both that there is a reasonable excuse for the lateness and that there is a stateable case to be made. The dispensing power has been used by a sheriff principal to relieve parties of the consequences of failure to appear at a hearing, although it was not disputed that the sheriff had quite correctly dismissed the action[4], and by another to excuse failure to intimate an appeal timeously to the respondents[5]. Once the court has dealt finally with a case and is *functus* so far as the proceedings are concerned, it is not possible to exercise the dispensing power. Thus, the sheriff who has granted decree has no power to recall the decree of his own motion[6] or to allow a party to appeal out of time, although the sheriff principal may do so[7]. Once the decree has been extracted, however, the sheriff principal cannot allow a late appeal[8].

1 *Calcranes Ltd v Aberdeen Northern Transport* 1978 SLT (Sh Ct) 52.
2 *W Jack Baillie Associates v Kennedy* above; *Alpine House Ltd v Links* above.
3 *Arshad v Scottish Power* 1992 SCLR 189.
4 *Webster Engineering Services Ltd v Gibson* 1987 SLT (Sh Ct) 101; but cf *Swan v Blaikie* 1992 SCLR 405.
5 *Renfrew District Council v Gray* 1987 SLT (Sh Ct) 70.
6 *Chris Hart (Business Sales) Ltd v Rome* 1993 SCLR 147.
7 *Hardy v Robinson* 1985 SLT (Sh Ct) 40; *McChristie v EMS Promotions Ltd* 1991 SLT 934.
8 *Alloa Brewery Co Ltd v Parker* 1991 SCLR 70; *Database Publications plc v McQueen Ltd* 1990 SLT (Sh Ct) 47; *Miro Windows Ltd v Mrugala* 1990 SLT (Sh Ct) 66.

8 THE HEARING

NATURE AND CONDUCT OF THE HEARING

8.01 The hearing is commonly referred to as the 'full hearing', in order to distinguish it from the preliminary hearing. It is also sometimes referred to as 'the proof', which is misleading if it is thought that it should necessarily resemble an ordinary or even a summary cause proof. Rule 19 applies to the hearing so that it 'shall be conducted in public in such manner as the sheriff considers best suited to the clarification of the issue before him; and shall, so far as practicable, be conducted in an informal manner[1]'. Virtually the only limits on the sheriff's discretion as to the form of enquiry are that any party to a small claim is entitled to give and lead evidence[2] and that such evidence, from a party or witness shall be given on oath or affirmation[3]. Further, no enactment or rule of law relating to admissibility or corroboration of evidence before a court of law is binding in a small claim[4]. This now refers to the few rules which are left after the passing of sections 1 and 2 of the Civil Evidence (Scotland) Act 1988 (c 21). It is to be noted that the right 'to give and lead evidence' does not necessarily imply a right to cross-examine the opposing party or his witnesses and it is a right which a party may or may not seek to exercise. It is perfectly acceptable for the sheriff simply to have an informal discussion of the disputed issues with the parties, perhaps making reference to documentary or other productions.

---

1 As to informality, see para **6.04** below; in *McGregor Associates v Greene* 1992 GWD 33-1970 the formal approach seems to have been preferred.
2 r 16(1).
3 r 16(3); cf *McLaughlin v Timber Terminal Ltd* 1993 GWD 6-436.
4 Sheriff Courts (Scotland) Act 1971 (c 58), s 35(2).

8.02   In *Dunn v David A Hall Ltd*[1] the agent for the defenders
apparently intended to lead evidence but claimed that he was so
taken aback when the sheriff decided to deal with the matter
simply by asking each agent to state his case that he made no
formal motion to lead evidence. On appeal, Sheriff Principal
Nicholson held that the sheriff was perfectly entitled to proceed in
that fashion in the absence of such a motion. He pointed out that 'it
is not for the sheriff to call for evidence to be led: it is for the party
wishing to lead evidence to do so'. The sheriff, however, had
overstated the situation in suggesting that rule 19 'gives the sheriff
carte blanche in deciding the manner in which the hearing is to be
conducted'. The sheriff may not decide a case in an injudicial
manner, or upon the basis of material which is plainly inadequate
to support any kind of decision. While the sheriff was entitled to
proceed as he did, it would be good practice for the sheriff to ask
the parties if they wish to insist on giving or leading evidence and
to note the replies[2]. It would also be inappropriate for the sheriff to
decide the case on a basis introduced *ex proprio motu* and on which
he has not been addressed[3]. The right to lead evidence is, of
course, a right to lead evidence relevant to the disputed issues and
the sheriff would be entitled and correct of exclude any evidence
which is not so relevant.

EVIDENCE

Witnesses

8.03   Where witnesses are called to give evidence, it would be a
matter for the sheriff to decide which witnesses to hear first. Each
party is responsible for the attendance of his witnesses and is
personally liable for their expenses[4]. The recovery of such
expenses by a successful party is subject to the limits prescribed in
rule 26 and might not, therefore, be recovered. The witnesses
must be cited not less than seven days before the hearing, the
summons or the copy of it served on the defender being sufficient

---

1 1990 SCLR 673.   2 Cf. also *Mannifield v Walker* 1990 SCLR 369.
3 *Hamilton District Council v Lennon* 1990 SLT 533.   4 r 16(1).

warrant for such citation[1]. The form of citation of the witness is form N and the certificate of execution thereof is form O in the summary cause rules. In terms of the summary cause rules these forms require to be signed by the party's solicitor or a sheriff officer and traditionally citation could only be done by a solicitor or sheriff officer. It is arguable that it is intended that the party should cite the witnesses himself in a small claim. This might seem to be a reasonable deduction from the terms of rule 16(1), the general intention that parties should be able to act for themselves and the lack of any provision, such as applies to service of the summons, intimation of incidental applications and recovery of documents, that the sheriff clerk should cite witnesses in some cases. On the other hand, the ordering of a witness to attend court, with the possibility of a finding of contempt of court for failure to do so, is a power which has to be exercised with such discretion that one would not expect to see it given to someone other than an officer of the court. It is submitted that, in the absence of clear provision to the contrary, only solicitors and sheriff-officers can cite witnesses. If the witness fails to answer the citation after having been properly cited and offered his travelling expenses if he has asked for them, he may be ordered by the sheriff to pay a penalty not exceeding £250 unless a reasonable excuse is offered and sustained. Payment of such penalty may be ordered to be made in favour of the party for whom the witness was cited[2]. The sheriff may also grant a warrant to compel the attendance of a witness under pain of arrest and imprisonment until caution can be found as the sheriff may require for his due attendance. The warrant is effective in any sheriffdom without endorsation and the expenses thereof may be awarded against the witness[3]. However, if a witness fails to appear the hearing will not be adjourned solely on that ground unless the sheriff on cause shown so directs[4]. Where evidence is given, the sheriff must make notes of the evidence for his own use which he must retain until after any appeal has been disposed of[5].

Productions

8.04 A party who intends to found at a hearing (other than a preliminary hearing) upon any document or articles in his possession,

---

1 SC r 29.   2 SC r 31.   3 SC r 32.
4 r 16(2).   5 r 20.

which are reasonably capable of being lodged with the court, shall lodge them with the sheriff clerk together with a list detailing the items no later than seven days before the hearing and shall at the time send a copy of the list to the other party[1]. The only documents or articles which may be used or put in evidence at the hearing, except if the parties consent or the sheriff permits otherwise, are documents which have been so produced or were produced at the preliminary hearing or have been produced under rule 18, which provides for the recovery of documents[2]. The provisions for recovery of documents and for replacement of lost documents have already been dealt with at paragraphs **7.10–7.13**. Solicitors may borrow productions, but a party litigant or a lay representative may do so only with the leave of the sheriff and subject to such conditions as the sheriff may impose. He may, however, inspect them within the sheriff clerk's office within normal business hours and may obtain copies, where practicable, from the sheriff clerk[3]. Once the hearing is concluded any documents or other productions referred to during the hearing and any report of a person to whom a matter has been remitted must be retained in the custody of the sheriff clerk until any appeal has been diposed of[4].

8.05 It has already been noted that, at the preliminary hearing, if a disputed issue noted by the sheriff is the quality or condition of an object, the sheriff may inspect the object in the presence of the parties or their representatives in court or, if it is not practicable to bring the object to court, at the place where the object is located[5]. The rule also applies 'at any subsequent stage of the small claim' so that the sheriff could follow that course at the full hearing[6]. Although the heading of rule 13 is *'Conduct of the preliminary hearing'* and there is no similar statement clearly extending the provisions of paragraphs (8) and (9) of the rule, it seems sensible to construe it as applying to them also, so that the sheriff could, if he considers it appropriate, at the full hearing, inspect any place material to the disputed issues in the presence of the parties or their representatives[7] or, on the joint motion of the parties, remit

---

1 r 17(1).   2 r 17(3).   3 r 17(2).
4 r 21.   5 See para **6.10** above.   6 r 13(7).
7 r 13(8).

to any suitable person to report on any matter of fact[1]. Taking either of these steps would, of course, almost certainly require an adjournment of the hearing.

Letters of request

8.06 Ordinary Cause Rule 28.14 is applied to small claims, making it possible to apply for evidence to be obtained outwith Scotland by an appropriate tribunal in another country. The application may be for the examination of a witness or for the inspection, photographing, preservation, custody, detention, production or recovery of, or the taking of samples of, or the carrying out of any experiment on or with, a document or other property, as the case may be[2]. The application must be made by minute in Form G16 together with a proposed letter of request in Form G17[3]. The letter of request is a document addressed by the sheriff to a foreign court or tribunal, requesting that court or tribunal to take the evidence referred to in the letter and transmit the record of it back to the applicant and, where necessary, it must be accompanied by an appropriate translation[4]. It is a condition of the granting of a letter of request that any solicitor for the applicant becomes personally liable for the whole expenses which may become due and payable in respect of it to the foreign court or tribunal and to any witnesses who may be examined for the purpose, and he must consign into court such sum in respect of such expenses as the sheriff thinks fit[5]. It is to be presumed that a party litigant in a small claim could make such an application, in which event the sheriff would no doubt require an appropriate sum to be consigned by the applicant. The letter of request, when issued, any interrogatories or cross-interrogatories, and any translation are forwarded by the sheriff clerk to the Foreign and Commonwealth Office or to such person and in such manner as the sheriff may direct[6]. Of course, since the formal rules of evidence do not apply to small claims, consideration should be given to any less formal means of obtaining such evidence as is required. Even an international telephone call to the witness by the sheriff should be cheaper.

---

1 r 13(9).   2 OC r 28.14(2).   3 OC r 28.14(3).
4 OC r 28.14(5).   5 OC r 28.14(4).   6 OC r 28.14(6).

INTIMATION OF DECISION

8.07 At the conclusion of the hearing, where practicable, the sheriff gives his decision, with a brief statement of his reasons, or he reserves judgment[1]. Where he reserves judgment he must give his decision in writing together with a brief note of his reasons within 28 days of the hearing. The sheriff clerk forthwith intimates the decision and note to the parties[2].

---

1 r 25(1).   **2** r 25(2).

9 DECREE

TYPES OF DECREE

9.01 The decree is the final order of the court by which the sheriff orders what is to be done in relation to the small claim. Rule 87 of the Summary Cause Rules, which provides that, where expenses are awarded, final decree is pronounced only after expenses have been dealt with in accordance with rule 88, is not applied to small claims but it seems unlikely that the position is any different in a small claim. The speciality is that rule 88 does not apply to every case[1] and expenses will normally be dealt with on granting decree[2]. Decree in favour of the pursuer will be as claimed or for part of the claim. Decree in favour of the defender can be in one of two forms, namely, dismissal or absolvitor. By decree of absolvitor the defender is, in old Scots parlance, assoilizied from the claim. That means that the dispute has been finally resolved in favour of the defender so that the pursuer cannot make the claim against him again[3]. If he tried to do so the defender could plead *res judicata* (the matter has been decided). Decree of dismissal falls short of a final decision. The court simply dismisses the summons from the court without ruling on the dispute. The pursuer may, therefore, seek to make the claim again in another process. This difference is so important that once a pursuer makes a claim, he cannot abandon it and ask for decree of dismissal rather than absolvitor unless he complies strictly with the terms of rule 22[4]. The decree, of whatever kind, may be a decree in absence, by default or on judgment given. It may be with or without expenses and if in favour of the pursuer, may or may not be subject to a time to pay direction.

---

1 r 26.   2 Cf r 25(3).
3 *Ross & Liddell Ltd v Ahmed* 1992 SCLR 528.   4 See para **7.15** above.

DECREE IN ABSENCE

9.02   Decree in absence is, properly speaking, always a decree in favour of the pursuer. It is granted where the defender makes no appearance at all. Any other decree, pronounced after the defender has appeared is, by contrast, a decree *in foro*. A party against whom decree in absence has passed may not have been aware of the claim having been made and is therefore entitled to have the decree recalled[1]. For these purposes rule 27 specifies the decrees which may be recalled and they are decrees granted in terms of rule 10(1)[2] and rule 13(1)[3]. Decree of absolvitor granted in terms of rule 13(3), against a pursuer who failed to attend the preliminary hearing[4] may also be recalled.

Recall

9.03   The important points to note in relation to recall of decree are that it may be sought only by parties against whom decree has been granted in terms of rule 10(1), rule 13(1) or rule 13(3), it must be sought timeously, by a minute, recall properly sought is granted as of right but the party may seek it on only one occasion. The pursuer against whom decree of absolvitor has been granted in terms of rule 13(3) may apply for recall of that decree by lodging with the sheriff clerk a minute for recall of decree in Form 14 within 21 days of the grant of the decree[5]. Where decree has been granted in terms of rules 10(1) or 13(1), the defender may similarly apply for recall not later than 14 days after the execution of a charge or execution of arrestment, whichever first occurs[6]. Where the defender is a partnership, a partner who is not sued as an individual is not a 'defender' and may not lodge a minute for recall[7]. It would seem likely that a sheriff could exercise the dispensing power in terms of rule 34[8] to allow a minute for recall of decree to be received late[9], but his decision one way or the other would not be a 'final decision' and, therefore, not subject to

---

1 r 27.   2 See para **5.07** above.   3 See para **5.08** above.
4 See para **6.02** above.   5 r 27(1).   6 r 27(2).
7 *A & E Russell Ltd v General Maintenance International* 1993 SLT (Sh Ct) 83.
8 See paras **7.16–7.18** above.
9 *Alpine House Ltd v Links* 1990 SLT (Sh Ct) 87.

appeal[1]. On the lodging of the minute, the sheriff clerk fixes a date, time and place for a hearing of the minute, which must then be served, together with a note of such time, date and place, by the party seeking recall upon the other party not less than seven days before the date fixed for the hearing.[2] Where the party seeking recall of the decree is not a partnership or body corporate or acting in a representative capacity and is not represented by a solicitor, the sheriff clerk must assist that party to complete and lodge the minute for recall[3], and must effect service on the other party either by first class delivery post or, on payment of the prescribed fee, by sheriff officer[4].

9.04 A minute for recall, when duly lodged and served, has the effect of preventing any further action being taken by the other party to enforce the decree[5]. On service on him of the copy minute, the party in possession of the summons must return it to the sheriff clerk[6]. At the hearing the sheriff must recall the decree, so far as not implemented and the small claim then proceeds in all respects as if the hearing were a preliminary hearing[7]. Presumably, if the summons were not returned in time for the hearing the sheriff would still be bound to recall the decree but might then dismiss the claim as in any other case where the summons was not timeously returned[8]. A party may apply for recall of a decree in the same small claim on one occasion only[9]. Where the party seeking recall failed to appear at the hearing on the minute and the minute was consequently treated as dropped, it was held that the party had not 'applied' for recall so as to render a later application incompetent[10]. Things were even more complicated in *Sureweld (UK) Ltd v D S Baddeley (Engineering) Ltd*[11] which was a summary cause in which the defenders initially failed to appear and decree in absence was granted against them. They lodged a minute for recall of the decree then failed to appear at the hearing and 'Accordingly no hearing took place'. The defenders' solicitors then lodged an incidental application 'to recall the minute for recall of decree . . .', under reference to the dispensing power. The sheriff

1 *W Jack Baillie Associates v Kennedy* 1985 SLT (Sh Ct) 53.
2 r 27(6).   3 r 27(4).   4 r 27(7).
5 r 27(10).   6 r 27(11).   7 r 27(8).
8 r 7(1); see para **4.16** above.   9 r 27(3).
10 *Alpine House Ltd v Links* above.   11 1987 SCLR 332.

refused the incidental application. On appeal the Sheriff principal (MacLeod) held that the sheriff's decision had been incompetent and was, therefore, appealable. The sheriff had no discretion but to grant recall, although he had been misled by the terms of the incidental application. Firstly, if application is made for recall, recall must be granted. Since recall had not yet been granted, it followed that application could not have been made. The incidental application was, in effect, an application for recall and since it was the first one and was also timeous it had to be granted. It is submitted that it was, in the first place, a mistake to say that 'no hearing took place'. It is also submitted that, where a minute for recall of decree is properly lodged and served the hearing must take place whether or not parties are present. The sheriff must recall the decree whether it is insisted upon or not. The hearing then proceeds in all respects as if it were a preliminary hearing, with the normal consequences in respect of failure to return the summons or failure to appear. Such an approach avoids the problems which have arisen in some of the reported cases. Had it been followed in *Sureweld (UK) Ltd* the decree would have been recalled in the defenders' absence but then decree would have been granted of new in terms of rule 13(1). This time, however, the defenders would not have been entitled to seek recall of the decree. The sheriff has no power to recall a decree of his own motion[1].

DECREE BY DEFAULT

9.05 A decree by default is one that is granted against a party who has put in an appearance but has failed to appear at a later stage or to perform some duty imposed by the rules or by the court. Such a decree cannot be recalled but may be appealed to the sheriff principal. Decree of dismissal against a pursuer for failure to minute for decree[2] or in respect of failure to return the summons[3] or decree of absolvitor in respect of failure to pay expenses timeously following an offer to abandon[4] are examples of decree by default. Decree by default is more commonly granted in respect of failure to appear at a hearing. Where all parties fail to appear or be

---

1 *Chris Hart (Business Sales) Ltd v Rome* 1993 SCLR 147.
2 r 10(2).   3 r 7(1).   4 r 22(4).

represented at any hearing, the sheriff must, unless sufficient reason appears to the contrary, dismiss the small claim[1]. Where one party does appear and the other does not the sheriff cannot grant decree by default without first fixing a special hearing in terms of rule 23[2].

DECREE ON JUDGMENT

9.06   The sheriff may grant decree following upon his decision on the merits of the case. That may be given at the preliminary hearing either by dismissing the claim as incompetent or because of lack of jurisdiction[3] or by granting decree of absolvitor or for part or all of the claim on the basis that the facts are sufficiently admitted for him to reach a decision[4]. Whether the judgment is given at the preliminary hearing or later after a full hearing the sheriff must first deal with the question of expenses and, where appropriate, make an award of expenses and grant decree as appropriate[5]. The decree then granted is a final decree[6]. He should not, however, deal with the question of expenses until after he has given his decision on the merits[7].

Time to pay direction

9.07   The circumstances in which it is open to a defender to make an application for a time to pay direction have already been dealt with at para **4.09** above and the procedure for making such application in a claim which is otherwise undefended at paras **5.06** to **5.12** above. The fact that a claim is defended does not, of course, preclude the making of an application for a time to pay direction in respect of any award that is made. Where a time to pay direction is competent the defender in a defended case may make a written or oral application to the court at any time before decree is granted for such a direction[8]. The same provisions described in chapter 5 in

---

1 r 23(5).   **2** See para **6.03** above.   **3** r 13(4).
4 r 13(6).   **5** r 25(3).   **6** r 25(4).
7 *Sloan v Mycock* 1992 SLT (Sh Ct) 23.   **8** r 24.

relation to time to pay directions in undefended cases apply to such directions in defended cases.

EXPENSES

Limits on awards of expenses

9.08 Section 36B of the Sheriff Courts (Scotland) Act 1971 provides that no award of expenses shall be made in a small claim in which the value of the claim does not exceed such sum as the Lord Advocate shall prescribe by order[1]. That sum is presently set at £200[2]. Further, the section provides that any expenses which the sheriff may award in any other small claim shall not exceed such sum as the Lord Advocate shall prescribe by order[3]. That sum is presently set at £75[4]. This means that where the small claim is for £200 or less, no expenses may be awarded in favour of one party against the other. Even where the claim is for more than £200 the maximum sum which can be awarded by way of expenses is £75. However, these limits do not apply to a defender who has not stated a defence, or has not proceeded with the defence stated or has not acted in good faith as to the merits of the defence. Where the sheriff granted decree at the preliminary hearing because he was unable to discern a relevant defence from what was said on behalf of the defender he correctly awarded expenses on the summary cause scale as the defender had not stated a defence[5]. They do not apply to any party on whose part there has been unreasonable conduct in relation to the proceedings or the claim nor do they apply in relation to an appeal to the sheriff principal[6]. A motion that the limits should not apply may be made orally upon the sheriff pronouncing his decision[7].

9.09 In fact, since the vast majority of small claims are not defended, the limits on awards of expenses will apply only to a

---

1 s 36B(1).
2 Small Claims (Scotland) Order 1988 (SI 1988/1999) art 4(2).
3 s 36B(2).   4 SI 1988/1999, art 4(3).
5 *Mutch v Payne* (31 August 1992, unreported), Aberdeen, per Sheriff Principal Ireland.
6 1971 Act, s 36B(3); cf *Milne v Uniroyal Englebert Tyres Ltd* 1994 GWD 7-407.
7 *Stewart Saunders Ltd v Gupta* 1992 GWD 28-1656.

minority of cases. The limitation will not apply, for example, to the position where a purported defence is rejected at the preliminary hearing as no defence at all[1]. Where a defence is accepted and a full hearing fixed but, prior to the hearing, the defender concedes the dispute and pays the sum claimed, the limitation does not apply, since he has not proceeded with the defence[2]. As was pointed out by Sheriff Principal MacLeod in *Gilmour v Patterson*[2], that does not encourage parties to proceed with useless defences nor discourage settlement. Settlement normally involves the resolution of expenses[3], while persistence in a defence once its lack of merit has been appreciated would be inconsistent with acting in good faith. In *Penman v North British Steel Group*[4] the small claim did not settle extrajudicially, but the pursuer's solicitors had refused to negotiate a settlement unless and until the defenders undertook to pay the pursuer's legal expenses. The pursuer sought £75 of expenses but the defenders sought modification on the ground that the pursuer's solicitors had been unreasonable in their attitude to the expenses and in declining to make available reports on the pursuer's medical condition to the defenders. It is somewhat difficult to see what the defenders were trying to achieve in the case or the relevance of reference to the tests for application of the limitations[5]. The pursuer was accepting that he should be awarded only £75. It is submitted, however, that the sheriff's suggestion that the rule relates to parties and not their solicitors and to proceedings in court and not to conduct of negotiations is in error. In any litigation parties are normally responsible for the conduct of their solicitors, as between themselves and the other parties, and unreasonable conduct 'in relation to proceedings' seems wide enough to cover more than proceedings actually in court. It has been held that where there are a multiplicity of parties the limitation to an award of £75 of expenses applies to the whole proceedings and not to each party, so that £75 was divided between the successful defenders[6].

---

1 Cf *Mutch v Payne*; *Hamilton v Ansah* 1990 SCLR 21 and para **6.05** above.
2 *Gilmour v Patterson* 1992 SLT (Sh Ct) 10; *Fenton v Uniroyal Englebert Tyres Ltd* 1994 SCLR 127; but cf *Hamilton v Sullivan* 1993 SCLR 969.
3 *Glover v Deighan* 1992 SLT (Sh Ct) 88.
4 1991 SLT (Sh Ct) 45.
5 As contained in the then current version of r 26.
6 *Sloan v Mycock* 1992 SLT (Sh Ct) 23.

Awards of expenses

9.10 Subject to the above limitations, the decision on whether to award expenses and in whose favour should be made on the same basis as in any ordinary action. It is always a matter for the discretion of the court. An award may be made in respect of any expenditure of expenses unnecessarily caused to one party, in whose favour the award is made, by the conduct of another party, against whom the award is made. Normally, accordingly, expenses are awarded in favour of the successful party, but it is not uncommon for that party to be found liable for expenses which were unnecessarily incurred. The most common example is, of course, where a pursuer is partly successful but the amount of the decree is less than what was offered in settlement by the defender at an earlier stage. The defender will then normally be awarded the expenses subsequent to the offer and the pursuer the expenses up to that point[1]. Where creditors obtained the warrant to serve but the debt was paid before service, the pursuers were held entitled to recover the court dues from the defender[2].

Procedure

9.11 Where an award of expenses has been made the sheriff clerk assesses the amount of the expenses in accordance with the statutory table of fees of solicitors appropriate to the summary cause, unless the sheriff otherwise directs[3]. The hearing is often referred to as a 'taxation', at which the sheriff clerk 'taxes' the amount of the expenses. Before doing so he must hear the parties or their solicitors on the claim for expenses including fees, if any, and outlays either in open court or in private[4]. This hearing should take place immediately upon the sheriff pronouncing his decision. Often, the parties should be able to agree a sum, or the amount appropriate can be assessed without difficulty, particularly if the

---

1 For a fuller exposition of the basis of awards of expenses see, eg MacPhail, *Sheriff Court Practice*, Chap 19.
2 *Clark & Rose Ltd v Mentiplay* 1989 SLT (Sh Ct) 66.
3 SC r 88(1); Act of Sederunt (Fees of Solicitors in the Sheriff Court) 1989, reg 3. cf. *Lothian Regional Council v Brown* 1992 GWD 39-2340.
4 SC r 88(3).

upper limit is £75. If, however, the sheriff so directs, or if he has reserved judgment, the hearing on the claim for expenses does not take place immediately but the sheriff clerk fixes a date, time and place when he will hear the parties or their solicitors in private. In that event, the successful party's account of expenses must be sent to the sheriff clerk and each of the other parties at least seven days before the hearing[1].

9.12 Unrepresented party litigants are not uncommon in small claims, and, if found entitled to expenses, such a party is entitled to outlays or expenses in terms of the Litigants in Person (Costs and Expenses) Act 1975 or any enactment under the Act[2]. The enactment to be referred to is the Act of Sederunt (Expenses of Party Litigants) 1976[3]. It provides that the sheriff clerk may allow to the party litigant as expenses such sums as appear to him to be reasonable having regard to all the circumstances in respect of (a) work done which was reasonably required in connection with the cause, up to a maximum of two-thirds of what would be allowable to a solicitor and (b) outlays reasonably incurred for the proper conduct of the case. The circumstances to which he does have regard must include the nature of the work, the time taken and the time reasonably required to do the work, the amount of time spent in respect of which there is no loss of earnings, the amount of any earnings lost during the time required to do the work, the importance of the cause to the party litigant and the complexity of the issues involved. A litigant who has been represented by an authorised lay representative may be awarded expenses on that same basis[4] as may a party so represented who is not an individual and could not have represented itself[5].

9.13 When the sheriff clerk has fixed the amount of the expenses he must report his decision to the sheriff in open court for the sheriff's approval. He must give intimation to the parties of the diet at which he is to report and the sheriff will hear the parties or their solicitors on any objections, after which he pronounces final decree including decree for expenses as approved by him[6]. Alternatively, the sheriff may, on the application of the successful party's solicitor, made at or before the time of the final decree being

1 SC r 88(4).   2 SC r 88(2).
3 SI 1976/1606, as amended by SI 1983/1438.   4 SC r 88(2A).
5 SC r 88(2B).   6 SC r 88(5).

pronounced, grant decree for the expenses in favour of the solicitor[1]. It is quite common for the sheriff clerk to intimate to the parties that the report will be made to the sheriff later on the day of the hearing on expenses. The intimation must be sufficient for the parties to have an opportunity to consider the taxation and to formulate objections[2]. Failure by any party to comply with any of the provisions of Summary Cause Rule 88 or failure by the successful party or parties to appear at the hearing on expenses must be reported by the sheriff clerk to the sheriff at the diet intimated to the parties, when the sheriff must, unless sufficient cause be shown, pronounce decree on the merits of the cause, finding no expenses due to or by any party, the decree then being a final decree[3]. Rule 23 would not, accordingly, apply to a failure to appear at a hearing on expenses, so that it would be inappropriate to fix a special hearing[4]. Late lodging of the account of expenses might result in no award being made[5]. It is possible, however, to ask the sheriff to exercise the dispensing power to excuse the late lodging. The relationship between summary cause rule 88(6) and the dispensing power was explained by sheriff principal Caplan:

'However what the rule says in clear terms is that there should be a good reason for not granting the decree. It does not stipulate that there should be a good reason for the default. . . . Rule 88(6) merely empowers the sheriff not to grant decree if sufficient cause for adopting that course is shown. It does not give him power to excuse default or make the necessary ancillary orders. . . . In my view para 5 and rule 88(6) are intended to co-exist. It follows in my view that a pursuer could apply to the sheriff to be relieved of a failure under rule 88(4) and that if such an application is presented it should be dealt with prior to the consideration of the rule 88(6) position since the grant or refusal of dispensation would be a material factor in deciding whether there was sufficient cause for not granting a decree[6].'

DECREE IN FAVOUR OF PERSONS UNDER LEGAL DISABILITY

9.14   In an action of damages in which a sum of money becomes payable, by virtue of a decree or an extra-judicial settlement, to or

1 SC r 88(7).   2 *Stewart Saunders Ltd v Gupta* 1992 GWD 28-1656.
3 SC r 88(6).
4 *Black Arrow Finance Ltd v Denniston Leisure* 1992 GWD 36-2161.
5 *McMillan v Webb* 1993 SLT (Sh Ct) 28.
6 *Colonel Gee Carpets Ltd v Watson* 1989 SLT (Sh Ct) 9; see also *Spax Ltd v Cook* 1992 GWD 39-2367; *Stevenson v Kinmund* 1990 SCLR 148.

for the benefit of a person under legal disability, Ordinary Cause Rules 36.14 to 36.17 apply. The sheriff makes such order regarding the payment and management of the sum for the benefit of the person as he thinks fit[1]. The sheriff may order the money to be paid directly to the person under legal disability or may appoint a judicial factor to invest or otherwise deal with it for his benefit, or may order it to be paid to the Accountant of Court or the person's guardian, as trustee to be applied, invested or otherwise dealt with and administered under the directions of the sheriff or he may order it to be paid to the sheriff clerk of the sheriff court district in which the person under legal disability resides, to be applied, invested or otherwise dealt with and administered under the directions of the sheriff of that district[2]. Where any such order is made, any person having an interest may apply for any later appointment, order or directions by a minute in the process[3]. At the request of any competent court the sheriff clerk must accept custody of any sum of money paid to him for these purposes[4]. A receipt in Form D2 by the sheriff clerk is a sufficient discharge in respect of the amount paid to him[5]. He deals with it appropriately only after such intimation, service and enquiry as the sheriff may order[6] and may invest it only in a manner authorised by the Trustee Investment Act 1961[7].

9.15 The disability may be by reason of insanity or non-age. If the insane person has a *curator bonis*, as would be usual, and who may well have raised the action, the court would usually simply pay to the *curator bonis*. In relation to a child under the age of 16, the sum of money payable in respect of a small claim will not be large and the court may very well simply pay it to the child's guardian to be applied on his or her behalf or even to the child, if old enough.

EXTRACT

9.16 An extract decree is, in effect, a certificate issued by the sheriff clerk showing that the decree has been granted and is

---

1 OC r 36.14(1).   2 OC r 36.15.   3 OC r 36.16.
4 OC r 36.17(2).   5 OC r 36.17(1).   6 OC r 36.17(3).
7 OC r 36.17(4).

necessary for enforcement of the decree. At any time before extract the sheriff may correct any clerical or incidental error in his interlocutor or note[1]. The extract of the decree signed by the sheriff clerk may be issued only after the lapse of fourteen days from the granting of the decree[2]. The sheriff has a common law power to supercede (ie delay the issue of) extract for a time but the power in Ordinary Cause rule 90(3) to allow early extract does not apply to small claims. The extract decree, which may be written on the summons or on a separate paper, may be in one of the appropriate forms appended to the summary cause rules and is warrant for all lawful diligence thereon[3]. The forms of relevance to small claims are Forms U1, U2, U2A, U9, U10, U11, U13 and U14. U1 is an appropriate form for an extract decree for payment. U2 is the same but including a time to pay direction for payment by instalments, while U2A includes such a direction for payment in a lump sum. Form U9 is a form for an extract decree for delivery of moveable property, while U10 is the same but including a warrant to search and open lockfast places. The court may grant such a warrant, to search for and take possession of goods and to open shut and lockfast places, when granting decree for delivery. Such a warrant applies only to premises occupied by the defender and may be executed only after the expiry of a charge following upon the decree for delivery[4]. Form U11 is appropriate to an extract decree for payment following upon failure to comply with a decree for delivery. Where the claim is for decree for delivery or recovery of possession of moveable property or for implement of an obligation, with an alternative of payment of a sum of money, the pursuer should seek decree for the first alternative in the first instance, specifying a time limit for compliance. Where there is failure to comply with that decree, he should then lodge an incidental application, which must be intimated to the defender, for decree in terms of the alternative crave for payment. He must appear at the hearing on such incidental application[5]. Form U13 is an extract decree of dismissal and Form U14 an extract decree of absolvitor.

---

1 SC r 89(4).   2 SC r 89(1).   3 SC r 89(2).
4 SC r 71.   5 r 41.

VARIATION ETC OF DECREE

9.17 Summary cause rule 92 applies to any case where the sheriff, *by virtue of any enactment*, may order a decree to be varied, discharged or rescinded or the execution of a decree to be sisted or suspended. The party requesting such an order must lodge a minute to that effect[1]. If such a minute is lodged by the pursuer he must also return the summons and extract decree, whereupon the sheriff clerk will grant warrant to cite the defender[2]. If it is lodged by the defender, the sheriff clerk grants warrant to cite the pursuer, ordaining him to return the summons and extract decree, and may, where appropriate, grant interim sist of execution of the decree[3]. At least seven days' notice of the hearing on the minute must be given, unless the sheriff on cause shown alters that period to one of at least two days[4]. Rule 92 does not apply to any proceedings under or subject to the provisions of the Debtors (Scotland) Act 1987[5], which would include proceedings relating to time to pay directions.

---

1 SC r 92(1).   2 SC r 92(2).   3 SC r 92(3).
4 SC r 92(4).   5 SC r 92(5).

10 APPEAL

WHEN COMPETENT

10.01 As in any summary cause, an appeal in a small claim lies to the sheriff principal on any point of law from the final judgment of the sheriff[1]. A fee (presently £26) is now payable on marking an appeal[2]. Unlike the position in any other summary cause, there is no further appeal to the Court of Session[3]. The separate provisions for appeal in relation to a time to pay direction are dealt with below[4]. The appeal must be from a 'final judgment', any other interlocutor not being subject to review[5]. Sheriff Principal Caplan examined the implications of this in three cases. In the first[6], he refused as incompetent an appeal against a refusal to adjourn a proof although, as a result of the refusal, decree was then granted of consent. The appeal was against an interlocutory judgment and was incompetent. As he put it:

'. . . the essential question in a summary cause appeal must be: "On the facts in the stated case did the sheriff err in law in pronouncing the final judgment (or any part of it)?"'

In that case, the final judgment was the granting of decree, which proceeded on an unopposed motion. In the second case[7], the sheriff had quite properly dismissed a summary cause when neither party appeared at the proof. The pursuers appealed, their solicitor seeking to tender an explanation for their failure to attend and inviting the sheriff principal to exercise the dispensing power to relieve them of the consequences. Sheriff Principal Caplan allowed the appeal, stating that:

---

1 Sheriff Courts (Scotland) Act 1971 (c 58), s 38(a).
2 The Sheriff Court Fees Order 1985 (SI 1985/827) as amended by SI 1993/2957.
3 1971 Act, s 38(b).   4 See below para **10.14**.   5 1971 Act, s 38.
6 *Rediffusion v McIlroy* 1986 SLT (Sh Ct) 33.
7 *Webster Engineering Services Ltd v Gibson* 1987 SLT (Sh Ct) 101.

'The words "from the final judgment of the sheriff" may suggest that the point of law requires to be one fundamental to the fabric of the sheriff's decision. However, I think that view may be unduly restrictive and that the application of the relevant stipulation can be applied to all points of law bearing upon the final judgment. . . . The effect of [s 38], in my view is to allow an appeal to the sheriff principal against any final judgment, provided that it is on a point of law. However, other appeals, that is to say appeals on questions of fact or on interlocutors which are not final judgments, are expressly disallowed.'

A final judgment must, however, be one which disposes of the issues between the parties. In the third case[1], decree in absence was granted against the defender. He sought to recall the decree but the sheriff refused to exercise the dispensing power to receive the minute late. It was against that refusal that the appeal was taken. On this occasion, Sheriff Principal Caplan said:

'A final judgment need not determine the merits of what is in issue between the parties but it must at least dispose of such issues. If a motion to recall a decree is refused it can in a sense be said to have a bearing on issues raised by the litigation for it is a refusal to interfere with the original disposal of these questions. However refusal to allow an extension of time is truly procedural in character and in no way can be said to have a direct effect on the issues of the case. . . . It follows in my view that the stated case does not raise a question of law arising from a final judgment so that the appeal is incompetent.'

Incompetent interlocutors

10.02 The restriction on appeal may not be applicable, however, if the interlocutor appealed against was itself incompetent in the sense that the sheriff had no power to grant it. The sheriff principal has an inherent power to correct incompetent procedure on the part of the sheriff. In an unreported case in Aberdeen Sheriff Principal Bell seemed to hold that that did not apply in summary cause procedure so that even an appeal against an incompetent procedural interlocutor was incompetent[2], and that seems to have been the view of Sheriff Principal Nicholson more recently[3]. Sheriff Principal MacLeod took a different view in Glasgow where,

---

1 *W Jack Baillie Associates v Kennedy* 1985 SLT (Sh Ct) 53, discussed in *Morton v N L Sperry Sun (UK) Ltd* 1994 SLT 13.
2 *L MacKinnon & Son v Coles*, 13 January 1984.
3 *City of Edinburgh District Council v Robbin* 1994 SCLR 43.

decree having been granted by default and expenses assessed, the defender appeared at the diet when the sheriff clerk's decision on expenses was reported to the sheriff[1]. The sheriff refused the pursuers' motion for decree and pronounced an interlocutor fixing a proof. The sheriff principal declined to follow Sheriff Principal Bell and allowed the appeal on the basis that an appeal against an incompetent interlocutor is always possible, a view which he had earlier applied in *Sureweld (UK) Ltd v D S Baddeley (Engineering) Ltd*[2]. It is submitted that that view is correct.

HOW MADE

10.03   The party who wishes to appeal may do so by lodging a note of appeal with the sheriff clerk not later than 14 days after the date of final decree. The note of appeal requests a stated case and must specify the point of law upon which the appeal is to proceed[3]. He must, at the same time as lodging the note of appeal, intimate its lodging to the other party[4]. Final decree is granted when the expenses have been dealt with[5]. All is not necessarily lost if there is a failure to comply with the above, as the sheriff principal may be persuaded to exercise the dispensing power in terms of rule 34, for example, to allow an appeal to be lodged late[6], or to relieve the appellant of the consequences of failure to intimate[7]. The application must be to the sheriff principal, as the sheriff, having pronounced final decree, is *functus* and can make no order[8]. Once decree has been extracted it is no longer open even to the sheriff principal to exercise the dispensing power and the appeal must be refused[9]. Where the extract itself is incompetent, however, as, for example, having been issued prematurely or after a late note of appeal has been lodged, the sheriff principal can take notice of the incompetency and apply the dispensing power[8]. In that context it

1 *City of Glasgow District Council v McAleer* 1992 SLT (Sh Ct) 41.
2 1987 SCLR 332.   3 r 29(1).   4 r 29(2).
5 r 25, see para **9.06** above.
6 *Hardy v Robinson* 1985 SLT (Sh Ct) 40; but cf *Anderson v Rollo, Davidson & MacFarlane* 1992 SCLR 797.
7 *Renfrew District Council v Gray* 1987 SLT (Sh Ct) 70. Cf *Guaranteed Trade Co v Melvin* 1993 GWD 11-790.
8 *Hardy v Robinson* 1985 SLT (Sh Ct) 40.
9 *Alloa Brewery Co Ltd v Parker* 1991 SCLR 70; *Database Publications Plc v McQueen Ltd* 1990 SLT (Sh Ct) 47; *Miro Windows Ltd v Mrugala* 1990 SLT (Sh Ct) 66.

has been noted that where a note of appeal is lodged late, the appellant should at the same time lodge an incidental application inviting the sheriff principal to exercise the dispensing power[1].

Abandonment

10.04   Once a note of appeal has been lodged by one party, any other party may take advantage of it, even if he has not lodged a separate appeal[2]. The other party may state any point of law he wishes to state in the appeal[3]. Accordingly, after he has lodged his note of appeal the appellant cannot simply change his mind and withdraw it. He requires the consent of the other party, which may be incorporated in a joint minute, or the leave of the sheriff principal, which may be subject to such terms as to expenses or otherwise as seems proper to the sheriff principal[2].

Interim possession and other orders

10.05   Pending the hearing of the appeal, the sheriff has power to regulate all matters relating to interim possession, to make any order for the preservation of any property to which the action relates or for its sale, if perishable, or for the preservation of evidence, or to make in his discretion any interim order which a due regard for the interests of the parties may require. Any such interim order may be reviewed only by the sheriff principal at the hearing of the appeal[4].

THE STATED CASE

Draft

10.06   Within 14 days of the lodging of the note of appeal, the sheriff must issue a draft stated case containing findings in fact and

---

1 *Anderson Brown & Co v Morris* 1987 SLT (Sh Ct) 96; *Millar v Millar* 1992 SLT (Sh Ct) 69.
2 SC r 82.   3 r 29(4)(b).   4 SC r 85.

law or, where appropriate, a narrative of the proceedings before him, appropriate questions of law and a note stating the reasons for his decisions in law. The sheriff clerk must, within those 14 days, send a copy of the draft stated case to the parties[1]. The narrative of proceedings would be appropriate to an appeal against a decision on procedural grounds, such as lack of jurisdiction or decree by default, where the facts are not established. However, even where no evidence is heard, as where the sheriff resolves the matter at the preliminary hearing, on the basis that the facts are sufficiently admitted, it would be better to set out these 'sufficiently admitted' facts. In *Mannifield v Walker*[2] Sheriff Principal Nicholson said:

'In the present case the stated case contained no express findings in fact and law but instead contained a narrative of what seems to have emerged during the hearing, followed by a note. In terms of rule 29(3)(a) . . . this approach is perfectly competent as an alternative to stating express findings in fact and law. However, . . . I have had difficulty in this case in determining exactly what facts the sheriff found to be proved and I suspect that there might have been no such difficulty had the sheriff followed the familiar practice of setting out specific findings. Given the alternative practice permitted by the rule . . . I do not go so far as to say that a sheriff should always state express findings in fact in a stated case. I consider, however, that it will be helpful if, by some means or another, a sheriff makes absolutely clear in a stated case what facts he found to be established.'

Where the decision on expenses is given at a later date from the merits, it could happen that more than one sheriff is involved in granting the final decree. To avoid the problems which could clearly arise on an appeal, it is, therefore, always preferable that the sheriff who dealt with the merits should deal with the report on the expenses. Where that does not happen, however, and appeal is taken on the merits and on the expenses then only one stated case should be prepared with each sheriff contributing a part[3].

10.07   In *Gilbey Vintners Scotland Ltd v Perry*[4] Sheriff Principal Bryden stated that:

'On the general question of how questions of law should be stated in a stated case under the new summary cause procedure . . . my view is that each such question ought to set out precisely and concisely a point of law to which the argument for the party stating the question will be directed at the hearing of

---

1 r 29(3).   2 1990 SCLR 369.
3 *Stewart Saunders Ltd v Gupta* 1992 GWD 28-1656.   4 1978 SLT (Sh Ct) 48.

the appeal. A question of law should not raise issues of fact or contain argument.'

It was further stated there that:

'This is the more important as the sheriff has no revising power and is required to state the questions as he receives them from the parties, however inept they may be.'

It is to be noted that this was in reference to the position under summary cause rule 81, which does not apply to small claims. In terms of small claims rule 29(7) it is quite clearly for the sheriff to formulate the questions, as it is provided that he must, in the stated case signed by him, include questions of law, framed by him, arising from the points of law stated by the parties and such other questions of law as he may consider appropriate[1]. Nevertheless, the above advice on their drafting would certainly apply.

Adjustment

10.08   Within 14 days of the issue of the draft stated case each party may lodge with the sheriff clerk a note of any adjustments which he seeks to make to the stated case and the respondent may state any point of law which he wishes to raise in the appeal. These must also be intimated to the other party[2]. The sheriff may allow a hearing on the adjustments and, indeed, must do so if he proposes to reject any proposed adjustments. He may also provide for such further procedure in relation to and prior to the hearing of the appeal as he thinks fit[3].

Signing

10.09   The sheriff must consider any note of adjustments and any representations made to him at any hearing on adjustments and, within 14 days of the hearing, or, if there was none, within 14 days of the latest date on which adjustments were or might have been lodged, state and sign the case[4]. Where the sheriff is temporarily

---

1 Cf *Milne v Uniroyal Englebert Tyres Ltd* 1994 GWD 7-407.
2 r 29(4).   3 r 29(5).   4 r 29(6).

absent from duty for any reason, the sheriff principal may extend the period allowed for issuing the draft or for signing the final stated case for such period or periods as he he considers reasonable[1]. In any event, such time limits are directory and not intrinsic to the sheriff's obligation and power to issue the stated case[2]. Lateness will not affect its validity. After the sheriff has signed the stated case, the sheriff clerk places all documents and productions in the small claim together with the stated case before the sheriff principal and sends to the parties a copy of the stated case together with a written note of the date, time and place of the hearing of the appeal[3].

CONDUCT OF THE APPEAL

Hearing

10.10 At the hearing the sheriff principal hears the parties on all matters connected with the appeal including liability for expenses[3]. If any party moves that the question of liability for expenses be heard after the sheriff principal has given his decision the sheriff principal may grant that motion[4]. A party is not allowed to raise questions of law of which notice has not been given except on cause shown and subject to such conditions as to expenses or otherwise as the sheriff principal may consider appropriate[5]. The sheriff principal will only hear a submission which is an argument in law and not something which is, in truth, an attempt to appeal on the facts. In *Kostric v O'Hara*[6] Sheriff Principal Mowat refused to answer the question:

'Had I exercised my discretion in such a manner as to arrive at a decision that no sheriff properly directing himself in law could properly have arrived at?'

as it appeared to open the question of the sheriff's assessment of the evidence. He also had doubts about the propriety of dealing with a question on the sheriff's interpretation of the Sale of Goods

1 r 29(6A). 2 *McMillan v Cavanagh* 1987 GWD 30-1143.
3 r 29(8). 4 SC r 83(1).
5 r 29(9), cf *McFall v Lochgorm Warehouses* 1978 SLT (Sh Ct) 67; *Verrico v George Hughes & Son* 1980 SC 179.
6 1990 SCLR 129.

Act 1979, when the interpretation of the Act had never been noted as a disputed issue, although he did deal with it. There would seem to be no reason why he could not do so 'on cause shown' in terms of rule 29(9). The sheriff's findings-in-fact may not be challenged and it is not open to try to undermine them by reference to his appended note[1].

Disposal

10.11   At the conclusion of the hearing the sheriff principal may either pronounce his decision or reserve judgment in which latter case he must give his decision in writing within 28 days and the sheriff clerk must forthwith intimate it to the parties[2]. The sheriff principal may adhere to or vary the decree appealed against or recall it and substitute another therefore or, if he considers it desirable, he may remit to the sheriff for any reason other than to have further evidence led[3]. It is thought, with respect, that the sheriff principal must have overlooked that latter provision in *North of Scotland Hydro-Electric Board v Braeside Builders' Trs*[4] when he remitted the case to the sheriff to allow adjustment of the disputed issues and to hear such further evidence as the parties wished to lead. It may be that, although he did not say so, he was following his predecessor who, in *Jamieson v Stewart (No 2)*[5], held that the reference to 'further evidence' should be construed in a restricted sense and did not prohibit further evidence where, through error on the part of the sheriff, a party had been prevented from leading proper evidence which was the cornerstone of his proof. In *McLaughlin v Timber Terminal Ltd*[6] the sheriff principal allowed the appeal and remitted to the sheriff for rehearing, but since that was on the basis that the sheriff had not properly heard the evidence at all, having failed to put the witnesses on oath[7], he was not remitting for 'further evidence'. In *Stewart Saunders Ltd v Gupta*[8], the sheriff principal dealt with an appeal on the merits and an appeal on the question of expenses. He allowed the appeal on the expenses and remitted to the sheriff to deal with the expenses

---

1 *KHR Financing Ltd v Jackson* 1977 SLT (Sh Ct) 6.   2 SC r 83(4).
3 SC r 83(3); *Scottish Homes v Rice* 1993 SCLR 380.   4 1990 SLT (Sh Ct) 84.
5 1989 SLT (Sh Ct) 30.   6 1993 GWD 6-442.   7 As required by r 16(3).
8 1992 GWD 28-1656.

in terms of summary cause rule 88(5). Since that meant that there was now no final decree, he was unable to deal with the appeal on the merits.

Expenses

10.12   The sheriff principal deals with the question of liability for expenses and may, on the motion of any party, hear the parties on that after he has given his decision[1]. The limits on the awarding of expenses in small claims do not apply in relation to appeals to the sheriff principal[2]. Otherwise, assessment of the expenses awarded at the appeal is dealt with in the same way as for decree at first instance[3]. When the sheriff clerk reports his decision on expenses to the court, the sheriff may pronounce the final decree on behalf of the sheriff principal[4].

TIME TO PAY DIRECTIONS

Application incompetent at appeal

10.13   Two questions occur in relation to appeals and time to pay directions. The first is the question of what happens if no direction has been sought before the sheriff but is sought from the sheriff principal at appeal. The second question is that of an appeal against the decision of the sheriff on an application for a time to pay direction. On the first point, it seems clear that if no application has been made to the sheriff, it is too late to seek a direction from the sheriff principal at appeal[5]. Section 1(1) of the Debtors (Scotland) Act 1987 allows the court to make such a direction 'on granting decree for payment'. The small claims rules allow for an application for a time to pay direction to be made 'at any time before decree is granted[6]'. There is no provision for an application at any later stage. It might be competent, however, where the

---

1 SC r 83(1).   2 Sheriff Courts (Scotland) Act 1971 (c 58), s 36B(3).
3 See paras **9.11–9.13** above.   4 SC r 88(5).
5 *Watson v McHugh* 1992 SLT (Sh Ct) 35.   6 r 24.

appeal is against decree of dismissal or absolvitor and the sheriff principal allows the appeal and grants decree for payment for the first time.

Appeal against a decision on time to pay direction

10.14   Where an application is made to the sheriff for a time to pay direction, or for variation or recall of such, it is possible to appeal against his decision, but only on a point of law and only with the leave of the sheriff. Such an appeal is not governed by section 38 of the Sheriff Courts (Scotland) Act 1971[1], but is in terms of section 103 of the Debtors (Scotland) Act 1987[2]. The application for leave to appeal must be made in writing, within seven days of the decision to be appealed against, to the sheriff who made it and it must specify the point of law on which the appeal is to proceed[3]. The appeal must be lodged and intimated to the other party within a period of 14 days from the date when leave to appeal was granted and the sheriff must state in writing his reasons for his original decision[4]. Notwithstanding an appeal, the decision of the sheriff takes immediate effect and remains in effect pending the appeal[5] and no appeal decision reversing the sheriff's decision can have retrospective effect[6]. Presumably, since there is no contrary provision, appeal is to the sheriff principal and/or the Court of Session, but even if a party were enthusiastic enough about a point of law on a time to pay direction on a small claims decree, it is to be anticipated that the sheriff would be less enthusiastic about granting leave to appeal to the Court of Session. The appeal to the sheriff principal proceeds in accordance with summary cause rule 83(1), (3) and (4)[7].

---

1 1971 (c 58).   2 1987 (c 18).   3 SC r 85A(3).
4 1987 Act, s 103(2); SC r 85A(4).
5 1987 Act, s 103(4).
6 Ibid, s 103(5).
7 See paras **10.11** and **10.12** above.

11 ENFORCEMENT

WHY A CHAPTER ON ENFORCEMENT

11.01 It could be said that a book dealing with small claims procedure is complete having dealt with all aspects of the procedure up to and including decree and appeals. Methods of enforcement of the decree, collectively referred to as 'diligence', are complex and generally cannot be used by a party litigant himself. It would be impossible in one chapter of a book of this kind to come close to a full explanation of the law and practice of diligence, which deserves a book to itself. Those who require a full explanation are referred to just such a book by G Maher and D J Cusine[1]. It is clear, however, that the perception of the members of the public who use small claims procedure is that enforcement is an integral part of the procedure. They express surprise and disappointment that the obtaining of a decree against the defender is not an end of the matter. They are, of course, correct in that the only successful conclusion to an action for payment is payment. Anything else may simply amount to throwing good money after bad and, therefore, anyone who is considering making a small claim in the sheriff court should consider carefully whether there is any point in raising an action against someone who is never going to be in a position to pay the decree. This simply underlines the advice that it is good practice before starting any proceedings to think things all the way through to the end, in order to foresee difficulties and to try to ensure a satisfactory conclusion. In that respect, this chapter might even be better at the beginning of the book than at the end.

11.02 A Central Research Unit paper, describing findings on research into the effectiveness of the small claims procedure,

---

1 G Maher & D J Cusine: *The Law & Practice of Diligence*, (Butterworths, 1990).

following on interviews with pursuers, defenders, advisers, sheriffs and court staff, found a number of pursuers who mentioned enforcement as 'the worst aspect of the procedure'. One pursuer had obtained a decree for £700 plus interest at 15 per cent plus £22 of expenses. He had then paid £168.73 to sheriff officers, who carried out an arrestment which produced nothing and a poinding which showed insufficient possessions to make a warrant sale worthwhile. At the end he had still not received anything[1]. Little wonder that he stated that the procedure was:

'an expensive and inefficient way to attempt to recover money. There is no point in the sheriff presiding over this if it does not come to anything . . . If the sheriff and the sheriff officer cannot do anything, it makes a monkey of the whole system.'

It is, unfortunately, a familiar story to those practising in the courts but not to the parties. Similar evidence came from lay advisers and court staff[2]. The comment and recommendation of the researchers was:

'The enforcement of decrees was a significant problem for successful pursuers who seemed to think that once success had been achieved the courts would enforce the decision. Half of the lay advisers said that enforcement problems were commonplace . . . and court staff noted that they were not infrequently asked for advice by successful pursuers about how to begin diligence procedures . . . .

T. This suggests that more information should be provided in the small claims booklet about the problems typically associated with enforcement, including the debtor absconding or having insufficient means to satisfy the decree. This should be clearly spelled out to potential pursuers prior to their raising an action. In addition, post-decree leaflets similar to the information sheets currently used in one of our study courts would be of value[3].'

11.03 If the pursuer who has obtained his extract decree[4] is fortunate, the defender will be willing and able to pay him without further trouble. The first step should be to write to him, pointing out that decree has been granted and that payment must be made

---

1 'Small Claims in the Sheriff Court in Scotland: An assessment of the use and operation of the procedure.' Scottish Office Central Research Unit Paper, 1991, chapter 4, paras 54–57.
2 Ibid, chapter 5, para 20 and chapter 7, paras 29–31.
3 Ibid, chapter 9, para 22, recommendation T.
4 As to which, see para **9.16** above.

within a stated time, failing which steps will be taken to enforce the decree, with increased expense and inconvenience to the debtor, and advising him on how and what to pay. If he does not pay, however, the extract is warrant for all lawful diligence thereon[1]. The next step would normally be to serve a charge to pay[2], though that is not a necessary preliminary to arrestment. The pursuer may seek to enforce payment out of moveable property belonging to the debtor in the hands of a third party by arrestment, followed by an action of furthcoming, or out of his earnings in the hands of the debtor's employers by an earnings arrestment or out of the moveable property of the debtor in his own possession by a poinding, followed by a warrant sale. The debtor, however, may be willing and simply unable to pay. The law will not allow him to be deprived of the essentials of life and, therefore, provides him with certain rights, including the right to seek a time to pay order.

TIME TO PAY ORDERS

When competent

11.04 As already described, the Debtors (Scotland) Act 1987 allows a defender who is an individual, liable for the debt either personally or as a guardian, judicial factor or *curator bonis* for an individual, to apply to the court for a time to pay direction at any time prior to decree[3]. If the debtor was not granted a time to pay direction prior to decree and is unable to pay at once, all is not yet lost, as the Act also allows him to apply for a time to pay order where, following on decree, a charge for payment has been served on him, or an arrestment has been executed or an action of adjudication for debt has been commenced[4]. By such an order the sheriff may specify that the debt shall be paid by specified regular instalments or as a lump sum at the end of a specified period[5]. The restrictions on making the order which might be relevant to a small claims decree are that it is not competent in relation to a debt including an amount of rates or taxes or where a time to pay

---

1 SC r 89(2).   2 See para **11.15** below.
3 1987 c 18, ss 1–4 and 14(1); see paras **5.06–5.12** above.
4 1987 Act, s 5(1).   5 Ibid, s 5(2).

direction or a time to pay order has previously been made[1] or a time order has previously been made under section 129(2)(a) of the Consumer Credit Act 1974[2]. Further, if the diligence has proceeded to an advanced stage, it is not competent to make a time to pay order in respect of the debt until the diligence has been completed or has otherwise ceased to have effect[3].

Application

11.05 Application for a time to pay order must be made to the sheriff court which granted the decree[4] by completing and lodging with the sheriff clerk an application in Form 2 in the Schedule to the Act of Sederunt (Proceedings in the Sheriff Court under the Debtors (Scotland) Act 1987) 1988[5]. The application must state, to the best of the debtor's knowledge, the amount of the debt outstanding and must include an offer to pay by instalments or by a lump sum at the end of a specified period[6]. He must also specify in the application whether a time order within the meaning of the Consumer Credit Act 1974 has been made in relation to the debt[7]. This requirement seems to have been forgotten in drafting Form 2, which contains no such statement. No fees are payable to the court in respect of the application and the sheriff clerk has a duty, if asked, to provide information as to the procedures and to assist the debtor in completion of the form[8], in accordance with the proposals for payment made by the debtor[9]. The sheriff clerk is not intended to take on the role of debt counsellor. However, while the sheriff clerk's staff are not obliged to give advice of this kind, the CRU Paper reported one sheriff clerk depute as saying that he thought it only sensible to offer the benefit of his experience, stating:

'They are looking for staff experience of what would be acceptable. I let them suggest a figure and then discuss it. I think its [*sic*] right to offer some advice on this[10].'

---

1 Ibid, s 5(4).   2 Ibid, s 14(3).   3 Ibid, s 5(5).
4 Ibid, s 15(3).   5 SI 1988/2013, r 5(1).   6 1987 Act, s 6(1).
7 SI 1988/2013, r 7(2).   8 1987 Act, s 96.   9 Ibid, s 6(2).
10 Small Claims in the Sheriff Court in Scotland: An assessment of the use and operation of the procedure. Scottish Office Central Research Unit, 1991, chapter 7, para 33.

This would appear to be a perfectly reasonable and fairly common approach, though not one that is demanded by the Act. Form 2 is not dissimilar to Figure 3 at para **5.06** above, and the advice given there is applicable here.

Procedure

11.06 On receipt of an application for a time to pay order, if it is properly made and unless it appears to him that the making of the time to pay order would not be competent, the sheriff must make an interim order sisting diligence[1]. Where the debtor is unable to furnish the necessary information, the sheriff may also make an order requiring the creditor to furnish such information as the sheriff considers necessary to enable him to determine the application[2]. The sheriff clerk serves a copy of the application on the creditor, together with a copy of any interim order sisting diligence and any order requiring information[3].

11.07 The creditor has 14 days after such service to object to the granting of the application or to make any counter-proposals[4]. If he fails to comply with an order to furnish information the sheriff, having given him an opportunity to make representations on the matter, may make an order recalling or extinguishing any existing diligence and interdicting the creditor from executing diligence for the recovery of the debt[5]. If no written objections are received timeously from the creditor the sheriff must make a time to pay order in accordance with the application[6]. If the debtor accepts a counter-proposal, the sheriff then grants a time to pay order in terms of the counter-proposal[7].

11.08 If agreement is not reached, the sheriff hears the parties and decides on the matter[8]. Where the time to pay order is refused, the sheriff recalls any interim order sisting diligence[9]. The sheriff

---

1 1987 Act, s 6(3); the effect of the interim order is detailed in s 8.
2 Ibid, s 6(4) and SI 1988/2013, r 5(2).   3 1987 Act, s 6(6); r 5(3).
4 SI 1988/2013, r 5(5).   5 r 5(4); 1987 Act, s 6(5).
6 1987 Act, s 7(1); SI 1988/2013, r 5(6).
7 r 5(8).   8 r 5(7).
9 1987 Act, s 7(3).

clerk intimates the decision to the parties, advising the creditor of the date when intimation was made to the debtor[1], as the time for the debtor to pay does not begin to run until such intimation to him[2]. The same provisions as to appeal apply as to an appeal in respect of a time to pay direction[3]. While a time to pay order is in effect it is not competent to serve a charge for payment or to commence or execute an arrestment and action of furthcoming or sale, a poinding and sale, an earnings arrestment or an adjudication for debt to enforce payment of the debt concerned. Existing diligences in respect of the debt are recalled or restricted or halted from further procedure[4]. There are similar provisions in respect of interest as apply in respect of a time to pay direction[5].

Variation or recall

11.09   Either the debtor or the creditor may make an application to the court for variation or recall of a time to pay order or recall of a poinding or recall or restriction of an arrestment[6]. The sheriff clerk fixes a date for the hearing of the application and intimates the application and hearing to the debtor and creditor. The sheriff may vary or recall the time to pay order if he is satisfied that it is reasonable to do so and may order that any variation, recall or restriction granted shall be subject to the fulfilment by the debtor of such conditions as the sheriff thinks fit[7]. The sheriff clerk intimates any variation granted to the debtor and the creditor and the variation comes into effect on the date of such intimation[8]. Where it comes to the knowledge of the sheriff that a debt to which a time to pay order applies is being enforced by a diligence which was in effect when the time to pay order was made, he must give all interested parties an opportunity to be heard, after which he has a choice of recalling the time to pay order, thus allowing the diligence to continue, or making the order which should have been made when the application was granted[9].

---

1 Ibid, s 7(4); r 5(9).   2 Ibid, s 5(2).
3 As to which see para **10.14** above.   4 Ibid, s 9.
5 1987 Act, s 5(6)–(8); SI 1988/2013, r 3; see para **5.09** above.
6 1987 Act, s 10(1); SI 1988/2013, r 6, Form 3.
7 Ibid, s 10(1), (2).   8 Ibid, s 10(3).   9 Ibid, s 10(4).

Lapse of time to pay order

11.10   If the court has ordered the debtor to pay by one lump sum at the end of a specified period, and any part of it remains unpaid 24 hours after the end of that period, the time to pay order ceases to have effect[1]. If the order was to pay in instalments and the date for payment of one of the instalments arrives while the debtor is still at least two payments in arrears, the order ceases to have effect[2]. The order also ceases to have effect if any part of the debt remains outstanding at the end of a period of three weeks immediately following the day on which the last instalment was payable[3]. A time to pay order also ceases to have effect on the debtor's sequestration or granting a trust deed or entering into a composition contract for the benefit of his creditors[4], or on the death of the debtor or the transmission of the debt concerned to another person during the debtor's lifetime[5]. Where the time to pay order is recalled or ceases to have effect otherwise than by the debt being paid or extinguished or on the sequestration or insolvency of the debtor, the outstanding debt, including interest thereon, becomes enforceable[6].

ARRESTMENT AND FURTHCOMING

Nature of arrestment

11.11   Arrestment is a diligence used against moveable property belonging to the debtor but which is not in his possession. The debtor's property is, accordingly, arrested in the hands of a third party. The creditor is referred to as the arrester, the third party in possession of the property as the arrestee and the debtor as the common debtor. Reference has already been made to arrestment on the dependence at paras **4.04–4.05** above. Arrestment used to enforce a decree is referred to as arrestment in execution of decree. It is made by service of a schedule of arrestment on the arrestee by a sheriff officer. The warrant giving authority to do so is the

---

1 Ibid, s 11(3).   2 Ibid, s 11(1).   3 Ibid, s 11(2).
4 Ibid, s 12(2).   5 Ibid, s 14(2).   6 Ibid, s 9(12).

warrant in the extract decree 'for all lawful execution hereon'[1]. The warrant may be executed anywhere in Scotland[2]. Where there has been arrestment on the dependence and the action is concluded in favour of the arrester, the arrestment on the dependence continues in force and, effectively, becomes an arrestment in execution. Arrestment is an inchoate diligence which establishes a *nexus* or attachment over the arrested goods or funds[3]. What this means, in effect, is that the funds or goods are 'frozen' in the hands of the arrestee, who is prohibited from voluntarily paying the debt or delivering the goods arrested to the common debtor or any other party. The arrester gets no right to the property and, if the common debtor does not agree to the arrestee releasing the property to the arrester in payment or part payment of the debt, the arrester must follow up the arrestment with an action of furthcoming to obtain a right to payment out of the arrested property.

Arrestable property

11.12 If the property is in the hands of the debtor arrestment cannot be used. The appropriate diligence is poinding. Normally, arrestment is not appropriate if the property is in the hands of the creditor. If, however, the creditor holds the property in a different character, eg as trustee for the debtor, from that in which he claims payment of the debt, he may arrest in his own hands[4]. That apart, the property will normally be in the hands of a third party and it must be moveable property. The kinds of property normally arrested include money due, such as money at credit in a bank account, rent payable by a tenant, claims for damages or under insurance policies or a bequest or the balance due by a building society which sold a house under a standard security and had more than enough to pay its debt[5] or shares in a company. Any goods held for delivery, such as by a seller to the debtor, or for repair,

---

1 Sheriff Courts (Scotland) Extracts Act 1892 (55 & 56 Vict c 17), s 7(1), as amended by the Debtors (Scotland) Act 1987, s 87(3).
2 1987 Act, s 91(1)(a).
3 Cf *Lord Advocate v Royal Bank of Scotland* 1977 SC 155, 1978 SLT 38.
4 Cf *Landcatch Ltd v Sea Catch plc* 1993 SLT 451.
5 *Abbey National Building Society v Barclays Bank* 1990 SCLR 639.

such as a car in a garage may be arrested and a ship should always be arrested rather than poinded. Among items of property which may not be arrested are earnings of the debtor in the hands of his employer. These are now subject to the new 'earnings arrestments' introduced by the Debtors (Scotland) Act 1987[1]. The latter Act also exempts a long list of items of clothing, tools of a trade, medical equipment, books, childrens' toys and normal and necessary items of household furniture and furnishings[2]. Alimentary payments and social security payments and state pensions are not arrestable. Funds appropriated to a particular purpose cannot be arrested so as to defeat the purpose of the appropriation. So, when an attempt was made to arrest a student's allowance in the hands of the Secretary of State, that part of the allowance referable to fees was not alimentary and therefore, in principle, arrestable, but since the Secretary of State had indicated to the university the intention of paying that part of the allowance directly to the university it could not be arrested, having been appropriated to that particular purpose[3].

Furthcoming or sale

11.13 When a creditor has succeeded in arresting property belonging to the debtor, that is usually enough to force the debtor to pay or to grant a mandate to the arrestee to hand over to the creditor so much of the funds as will pay the debt, whereupon the creditor may release the remaining property arrested. If that does not happen, however, the creditor must proceed to an action of furthcoming. Such an action may proceed in the Court of Session or in the sheriff court as an ordinary action. The action is raised against both the arrestee and the common debtor and craves an order for the arrestee to make furthcoming, payment and delivery of the sum owed by the arrestee to the common debtor and arrested in his hands by the pursuer, or so much of it as will pay the debt and the expenses of the diligence. Where the property arrested consists of goods rather than money, the action may crave an order for sale of the goods and payment of the debt and expenses out of

---

1 See paras **11.21–11.23** below.   2 1987 Act, ss 16, 99(2).
3 *Hughes v Lord Advocate* 1992 GWD 35–2082.

the proceeds[1]. Payment of the full amount recoverable at any stage or a tender thereof which is not accepted within a reasonable time results in the diligence ceasing to have effect[2].

EARNINGS ARRESTMENT

New diligence

11.14   In relation to the earnings of a debtor in the hands of his employer, the Debtors (Scotland) Act 1987 introduced three new diligences, to be known, respectively, as an 'earnings arrestment', a 'current maintenance arrestment' and a 'conjoined arrestment order[3]'. These new diligences are quite different from the common law arrestment and furthcoming referred to in the previous paragraphs[4], which is no longer competent in relation to earnings[5]. A 'current maintenance arrestment' could not follow from a small claims decree. 'Earnings' and 'employer' are, for these purposes, defined in s 73 of the Act.

Charge for payment

11.15   An earnings arrestment is not competent unless a charge for payment has been served on the debtor and the period for payment has expired without payment being made[6]. A charge is a formal demand, in writing, served on the debtor, requiring him to pay the sum or sums stated to be due to the creditor within a specified time, failing which diligence may proceed against him. The charge must be served on the debtor by a sheriff officer. The period for payment specified in the charge must be 14 days if the debtor is within the UK or 28 days if he is outside the United Kingdom or his whereabouts are unknown[7]. The warrant for

---

1 As to expenses, see 1987 Act, ss 93, 94.
2 Ibid, s 95(1).   3 Ibid, s 46(1).
4 Cf *Scobie v Dumfries and Galloway Regional Council* 1991 SLT (Sh Ct) 33; *Slater v Grampian Regional Council* 1991 SLT (Sh Ct) 72.
5 Sheriff Courts (Scotland) Extracts Act 1892 (55 & 56 Vict c 17), s 7(1), as amended by the Debtors (Scotland) Act 1987, s 87(3).
6 1987 Act, s 90(1).   7 Ibid, s 90(3).

execution on the extract decree is warrant for the charge[1]. The form of the charge is given by Act of Sederunt[2]. Once the charge has been served and the period for payment has expired, unless payment is made, the creditor has the right to execute a poinding or an earnings arrestment up to two years after the service on the debtor[3]. A further charge for payment, before or after the expiry of the two years, may reconstitute the creditor's right to execute such diligence[4], but if the further charge is within two years of the first charge, no expenses incurred in the service of the further charge is chargeable against the debtor[5]. The sheriff officer must submit a report of the charge to the court, signed by both the officer and the witness to the charge. Where the defender's address is not known, service is in terms of ordinary cause rule 30.9.

Service of earnings arrestment

11.16   An earnings arrestment comes into effect upon the service by a sheriff officer of an 'earnings arrestment schedule', in the appropriate form on the debtor's employer[6], and remains in effect until the debt has been paid, or otherwise extinguished, the employment ceases or the arrestment has been recalled, abandoned or ceases to have effect[7]. The debt outstanding and recoverable may include the debt and expenses due under the decree, interest thereon accrued at the date of execution of the earnings arrestment and expenses of the execution and preceding charge, but only to the extent specified in the schedule[8]. Service is by registered or recorded delivery letter or, if such a letter cannot be delivered, by any other competent mode of service[9]. The officer serving must, if reasonably practicable, intimate a copy of the schedule to the debtor, though failure to do so does not itself render the arrestment invalid[10]. Unlike the common law arrestment, it is perfectly possible for the employer of the debtor, if he is a creditor, to make an earnings arrestment in his own hands[11].

---

1 Sheriff Courts (Scotland) Extracts Act 1892 (55 & 56 Vict c 17), s 7(1), as amended by the Debtors (Scotland) Act 1987, s 87(3).
2 Act of Sederunt (Form of charge for payment) 1988 (SI 1988/2059).
3 1987 Act, s 90(5).   4 Ibid, s 90(6).   5 Ibid, s 90(7).
6 Ibid, s 47(2)(a); SI 1988/2013, r 38, Form 30.   7 1987 Act, s 47(2)(b).
8 1987 Act, s 48.   9 Ibid, s 70(3).   10 Ibid, s 70(1), (2).
11 *Scobie v Dumfries and Galloway Regional Council* 1991 SLT (Sh Ct) 33; *Slater v Grampian Regional Council* 1991 SLT (Sh Ct) 72.

Effect

11.17   The general effect of an earnings arrestment is to require the employer to deduct a sum from the debtor's net earnings on every pay-day and to pay that sum to the creditor[1]. The amount of the sum to be deducted is calculated in accordance with s 49 and the tables in Schedule 2 to the 1987 Act. An employer who fails to comply with the arrestment will be personally liable to pay the sum which should have been deducted, without being entitled to recover from the debtor any sum paid to him in contravention of the arrestment[2]. Payment to the creditor may be by cheque but if a cheque tendered in payment is dishonoured, the creditor may insist on cash payments thereafter[3]. However payment is made, all parties should ensure that they have a reliable record of payments made in case of dispute at a later stage. On each occasion on which he makes a payment to the creditor, the employer is entitled to charge the debtor a sum, presently 50p, by way of fee and to deduct it from his net earnings[4]. No claim may be made by either the debtor or the creditor against the employer in relation to any deductions or payments which have or ought to have been made under an earnings arrestment order more than one year after the date when the deduction or payment has or ought to have been made[5].

11.18   An application for review of an earnings arrestment may be made to the sheriff having jurisdiction over the place where the earnings arrestment was executed or, if that place is unknown to the applicant, over an established place of business of the debtor's employer[6]. The debtor or any person on whom an earnings arrestment schedule has been served may apply to such sheriff for an order declaring that the earnings arrestment is invalid or has ceased to have effect[7]. If the sheriff is satisfied that the arrestment is invalid or has ceased to have effect, he must make the order, which is not subject to appeal[8]. The sheriff may, on an application by the debtor, the creditor or the employer, make an order determining any dispute as to the operation of an earnings

1 1987 Act, s 47(1).   2 Ibid, s 57(1).   3 Ibid, s 57(2), (3).
4 Ibid, s 71.   5 Ibid, s 69(4).   6 Ibid, s 73(1).
7 Ibid, s 50(1); SI 1988/2013, r 40, Form 32.   8 1987 Act, s 50(2).

arrestment[1]. Since the application must state the subject matter of the dispute and the form of order sought it is submitted that it is not enough, for example, for a creditor simply to complain that nothing has been paid. That does not indicate that there is a dispute. He should state the order he wishes to be made (ie how much he should be paid) and the justification for it (ie why he thinks he is entitled to it). Where the debt is paid in full or otherwise extinguished or ceases to be enforceable by diligence, the creditor must intimate that fact to the employer, in writing, as soon as is reasonably practicable[2]. Any sum paid by the employer in excess of the debt is recoverable by the debtor from the creditor with interest[3]. If the excess was paid as a result of the creditor failing to give timeous intimation to the employer, the sheriff, on an application by the debtor, may make an order requiring the creditor to pay up to twice the amount otherwise recoverable by the debtor[4].

Multiple arrestments

11.19 The general rule is that only one arrestment can be in force against the debtor's earnings at any one time[5], though it is competent for the same creditor to enforce more than one debt in the same earnings arrestment[6]. There is an exception where there is one earnings arrestment and one current maintenance arrestment. The employer must first operate the earnings arrestment on the net earnings and then the current maintenance arrestment on the balance[7]. Where the employer receives two or more arrestments on the same day the first to arrive is given effect or, if it cannot be said which was first, the employer chooses which one shall have effect[8]. The employer must advise any creditor whose arrestment is not given effect of the existence of the earlier arrestment, giving the name and address of the creditor, the date and place of execution and the debt recoverable in terms of the schedule[9]. The second creditor, being unable to make an earnings

1 Ibid, s 50(3); r 41, Form 33.
2 Ibid, s 57(4); r 50.
3 1987 Act, s 57(5).
4 Ibid, s 57(6); r 51, Form 41.
5 1987 Act, s 59.
6 Ibid, s 48(4).
7 Ibid, s 58.
8 Ibid, s 59(3).
9 Ibid, s 59(4).

arrestment, has the remedy of applying for a conjoined arrestment order.

CONJOINED ARRESTMENT ORDER

Application

11.20 A creditor who would have been able to execute an earnings arrestment but for the existence of an earlier earnings arrestment may apply to the sheriff having jurisdiction over the place where the existing earnings arrestment was executed[1] for a conjoined arrestment order[2]. The sheriff clerk intimates the application to the debtor, the employer and any creditor enforcing a debt by the existing earnings arrestment and any current maintenance arrestment[3]. If there is no dispute the sheriff may grant the application or make such other order as he considers appropriate. If an objection is made, there is a hearing. The sheriff must grant the order if the application is properly made[4], and his decision to do so is not subject to appeal[5]. A copy of the order is served by the sheriff clerk on the applicant, the employer, the debtor and other creditors[6]. It comes into effect 7 days after such service on the employer[7].

Effect

11.21 The order recalls the existing earnings arrestment and requires the employer to deduct a sum calculated in accordance with s 63 of the Act from the debtor's net earnings on any pay-day and to pay it to the sheriff clerk[8]. If the employer fails to comply with the conjoined arrestment order he will be liable to pay to the sheriff clerk any sum he would have paid if he had so complied, without being able to recover any sum paid to the debtor in contravention of the order and the sheriff may grant to the sheriff

1 Ibid, s 73(1).
3 1987 Act, s 60(7); r 53(3).
5 Ibid, s 60(8).
7 1987 Act, s 60(6)(a).

2 Ibid, s 60; r 53, Form 43.
4 1987 Act, s 60(2).
6 1987 Act, s 60(7); r 54, Form 45.
8 Ibid, s 60(3).

clerk warrant for diligence against the employer[1]. The sums received by the sheriff clerk are disbursed by him in accordance with the provisions of Schedule 3 of the 1987 Act, which, broadly, give ordinary debts priority over maintenance debts, the creditors on the ordinary debts getting shares proportionate to their respective debts[2]. The total amount recoverable by a creditor is similar to what could be recovered under an earnings arrestment[3].

Variation, disputes and recall

11.22 While a conjoined arrestment order is in operation, no other earnings arrestment is competent[4]. The employer must inform new creditors whose arrestments fall or fail to take effect which court made the conjoined order, failing which the sheriff having jurisdiction over the place where the new arrestment is served may order him to do so[5]. The remedy for a creditor who could have served an earnings arrestment but finds that he cannot do so because of a conjoined arrestment order is to apply to the sheriff who made the conjoined arrestment order for an order varying the conjoined arrestment order to include the new creditor's debt[6]. The sheriff may make an order determining any dispute on the operation of a conjoined arrestment order on the application of the debtor, a creditor, the employer or the sheriff clerk[7]. Any of those persons may also apply for a recall or a variation of the conjoined arrestment order[8]. If a time to pay order is made, the debt is taken out of the conjoined arrestment[9].

POINDING AND SALE

Nature of poinding

11.23 The diligence of poinding and sale is carried out by sheriff officers very much under the control of the court and now largely

1 Ibid, s 60(9); r 55.
2 1987 Act, s 64.
3 Ibid, s 61; cf para **11.17** above.
4 Ibid, s 62.
5 Ibid, s 73; r 56, Form 48.
6 1987 Act, s 62(5); r 57, Form 49.
7 1987 Act, s 65(1); r 59, Form 54.
8 1987 Act, s 66; rr 61–65, Forms 56 to 59.
9 1987 Act, s 9(2)(b).

governed by the provisions of the Debtors (Scotland) Act 1987. The diligence is used against moveable property, mainly goods, belonging to the debtor and in his own possession. The poinding renders the goods litigious, which means that, while the debtor retains the goods and can use them, he must not remove them from the premises where the poinding took place[1] nor wilfully damage or destroy them[2]. The creditor must then obtain a warrant for sale of the goods from the sheriff and, upon the sale of the goods, may obtain payment of the debt and expenses out of the proceeds. The warrant for the poinding, which may be executed anywhere in Scotland[3], is the warrant in the extract decree 'for all lawful execution hereon[4]'. A poinding must be preceded by the expiry without payment of the days of a charge for payment[5]. The poinding is carried out by a sheriff officer, who is accompanied by a witness, following the procedure set out in s 20 of the 1987 Act. He must value the articles poinded at what he considers to be their value on the open market and leave a poinding schedule, signed by himself and the witness, for the debtor[6]. Thereafter, he must report to the sheriff on the execution of the poinding within 14 days (or later if allowed)[7]. The report must be to the sheriff for the place where the decree is being enforced (ie where the poinding takes place)[8].

Property poindable

11.24   Poinding is followed by a sale and, therefore, it is generally only property which can be sold which may be poinded. Incorporeal property which probably includes money, is not poinded. Goods belonging to the debtor which are in the possession of the creditor may be poinded by the creditor. The 1987 Act exempts a long list of items of clothing, tools of trade, medical equipment, books, children's toys and normal and necessary items of house-

---

1 Ibid, s 28.   2 Ibid, s 29.   3 Ibid, s 91(1).
4 Sheriff Courts (Scotland) Extracts Act (55 & 56 Vict c 17), s 7(1), as amended by the Debtors (Scotland) Act 1987, s 87(3).
5 1987 Act, s 90(1); see para **11.16** above.
6 SI 1988/2013, r 11, Form 5.
7 1987 Act, s 22; r 15, Form 9.
8 *Bruckash Ltd v Lonie* 1990 SCLR 780.

hold furniture and furnishings, etc[1]. Section 26 provides protection for the debtor where a caravan, houseboat or other moveable structure is his only or principal residence[2]. Goods which do not belong to the debtor may not be poinded and, therefore, the procedure includes a duty on the sheriff officer to make enquiry of any person present as to ownership[3], although he is entitled to proceed on the assumption that any article in the possession of the debtor is owned by him[4]. He must not poind more than is necessary to ensure the debt recoverable would be met if the goods were sold at his valuation[5]. The debtor has 14 days to redeem any poinded article at the value fixed, which article cannot be repoinded[6].

Applications to the sheriff

11.25   The Act provides for a number of applications to be made to the sheriff. These include an application regarding the security of articles or disposal of articles of a perishable nature[7], for release of a poinded article on the ground of undue harshness[8], or because it is exempt[9], for declarator that the poinding is invalid or has ceased to have effect or for recall of the poinding on the ground of undue harshness or undervaluation or that the proceeds of sale are not likely to cover the expenses thereof[10]. A third party may apply for release of articles which belong to him[11] or are owned in common by himself and the debtor, on the ground of undue harshness[12].

Warrant sale

11.26   Within one year of the poinding or such longer time as the sheriff allows[13], the creditor may apply to the sheriff for a warrant

---

1 s 16.   2 Rule 18, Form 12.   3 s 20(2)(c).
4 s 19(2) and (3).   5 s 19(1).   6 s 21(4) to (6).
7 s 21(1) and (2); rules 12 and 13, Forms 6 and 7.   8 s 23; r 16, Form 10.
9 s 16(4); r 8, Form 4.
10 s 24; r 17, Form 11; for an example of undervaluation cf *MacIver v Strathclyde Regional Council* 1992 SLT 7.
11 s 40; r 34, Form 27.
12 s 41(3); r 35, Form 28; cf *McCallum* 1990 SLT (Sh Ct) 90.
13 s 27; r 19, Form 13; but cf *Primesight Bus Advertising Ltd v Canning and Crawford* 1990 SCLR 349.

of sale of the poinded articles[1]. A copy of the application is served on the debtor, who has 14 days to object. The warrant sale is by public auction arranged by an officer appointed and at a place and within a period specified in the warrant[2]. There are restrictions on the places where the sale may be held and, in particular, it should not be in a dwelling-house except with the consent of the occupier and the debtor[3]. The officer appointed must attend and see the sale conducted in accordance with the Act[4]. If the creditor fixes a reserve price it must not exceed the value fixed at the poinding and if it is sold for less than that value, the debtor is credited with the fixed value. The creditor is entitled to recover the amount outstanding under the decree together with the expenses of the charge and poinding and sale[5]. If that sum is not realised by the sale, ownership of any unsold goods passes to the creditor. If the sum recoverable is realised, the officer appointed pays that sum to the creditor and pays the balance to the debtor[6]. Within 14 days he must give a report of the sale to the sheriff for checking and approval or otherwise[7].

DEBTORS (SCOTLAND) ACT 1987 PROCEEDINGS

11.27 Applications for time to pay orders, earnings arrestments, conjoined earnings arrestment and proceedings relating to poinding and sale are all largely carried out in terms of the Debtors (Scotland) Act 1987. There are some general provisions of importance to all such proceedings. Any party is entitled to be represented by a person other than an advocate or a solicitor if the sheriff is satisfied that the person is a suitable representative and is duly authorised to represent the party[8]. Generally, no expenses are awarded, but if an application is frivolous or is opposed on frivolous grounds or a party requires a hearing on frivolous grounds, the sheriff may award up to £25 expenses against the party acting frivolously[9]. That does not apply in relation to expenses of poinding

---

1 s 30; r 26, Form 20.   2 s 31.   3 s 32.
4 s 37.   5 s 45.   6 s 38.
7 s 39; rr 31, 33, Form 26.   8 r 70.
9 s 92.

and sale, an application for a time to pay direction, an appeal or in relation to anyone other than the debtor and creditor. The debtor will not require to pay any fees to the court and the sheriff clerk will provide him with information as to the procedures and assist him in the completion of relevant forms[1]. Neither the debtor nor the creditor are entitled to legal aid, although a third party might be[2]. Appeals are restricted[3]. Failure to use the appropriate Forms or to follow the precise procedure is likely to render the proceedings invalid[4]. The sheriff has a dispensing power in relation to the rules in the Act of Sederunt similar to the dispensing power in the small claims rules[5].

CIVIL IMPRISONMENT

11.28 The remedy of imprisoning a debtor for failure to obtemper a decree of the court has been considerably restricted and is not available simply for failure to pay under a small claims decree for payment. It is, however, still available in respect of a failure to obtemper a decree *ad factum praestandum*. On an application to the court for a warrant for imprisonment, it is open to the court to recall the decree *ad factum praestandum* and to make an order for payment instead[6]. Since a small claim for a decree *ad factum praestandum* must always be accompanied by an alternative claim for payment[7], it would appear that the remedy for failure to comply with the decree *ad factum praestandum* is to take decree in the alternative. Civil imprisonment is not, therefore, available to enforce a small claim.

---

1 s 96; see para **11.05** above.
2 s 98.
3 s 103; sections dealing with particular proceedings frequently prohibit any appeal. For a successful appeal following on a fundamental flaw in the procedure see *Thom v Thom* 1992 SLT (Sh Ct) 20.
4 *Norris v Dumfries and Galloway Regional Council* 1991 SLT (Sh Ct) 30; *Scobie v Dumfries and Galloway Regional Council* 1991 SLT (Sh Ct) 33; *Douglas v Fife Regional Council* 1991 SLT (Sh Ct) 57; but cf *MacIver v Strathclyde Regional Council* 1992 SLT (Sh Ct) 7.
5 r 75; see paras **7.16–7.18** above.
6 Law Reform (Miscellaneous Provisions) (Scotland) Act 1940 (3 & 4 Geo 6, c 42), s 1; 1987 Act, s 100.
7 See para **4.01** above.

INHIBITION AND ADJUDICATION

11.29 Inhibition and adjudication are diligences enforced against the heritable property of the debtor and both require a warrant to be obtained by application to the Court of Session, even to enforce a sheriff court decree[1]. Inhibition, like arrestment, is a diligence which gives a security of sorts to a creditor by freezing the debtor's ability to deal with his property, without giving the creditor any right or title to any of the debtor's property. Like arrestment, it can be used on the dependence of an action as well as in execution. When served on the debtor and recorded in the Register of Inhibitions and Adjudications in Edinburgh, it prevents the debtor from disposing of or burdening any heritable property belonging to him in Scotland. Just as arrestment must be followed by an action of furthcoming, inhibition must be followed by adjudication to give the creditor any right to the debtor's property. Adjudication is, however, a separate diligence, which may proceed without a prior inhibition and which, again, may be used on the dependence or in execution. It proceeds as a special action in the Court of Session by which specified heritable property of the debtor is seized and 'adjudged' to the creditor, who completes title to the property by recording in the appropriate Register. While small claims may, in theory, be enforced by inhibition and adjudication[2], the latter, in particular, has been described as 'slow, cumbrous, archaic and obscure[3]' and is not recommended.

SEQUESTRATION

11.30 Sequestration is the process by which a debtor, who is unable to pay his debts, is declared bankrupt and his property taken over by a trustee appointed by the court, who realises all the assets of the debtor and pays the proceeds over to the creditors proportionally to their debts. Even if the debts are not paid in full

---

1 For a full explanation see G L Gretton, *The Law of Inhibition and Adjudication* (Butterworths/Law Society of Scotland, 1987).
2 *Gretton*, p 7.　　　3 *Gretton*, p 156.

the debtor is eventually discharged from further payment. The procedure, which is in terms of the Bankruptcy (Scotland) Act 1985 (c 66), recently amended by the Bankruptcy (Scotland) Act 1993 (c 6), may be in the Court of Session or in the sheriff court and may be sought by a creditor or creditors who are owed more than £1,500[1]. Accordingly, creditors under a small claims decree could probably not proceed on that basis alone and, in any event, if the debtor was not able to pay even a relatively small debt, the chances of a creditor getting much out of his sequestration would not be high. Nevertheless, the process seems to have commended itself to those seeking to enforce the community charge.

---

1 1985 Act, s 5(4), as amended by the 1993 Act, s 3(3).

APPENDIX

Small Claims Rules 1988

Ordinary Cause Rules 1993
applying to small claims

Summary Cause Rules 1976
applying to small claims

Small Claims Rules 1988

(SI 1988/1976)

1. Citation and commencement

(1) This Act of Sederunt may be cited as the Act of Sederunt (Small Claim Rules) 1988 and shall come into force on 30th November 1988.

(2) This Act of Sederunt shall be inserted in the Books of Sederunt.

2. Small Claim Rules

(1) The provisions of the Schedule to this Act of Sederunt shall have effect for the purpose of providing rules for the form of summary cause process known as a small claim under section 35(2) of the Sheriff Courts (Scotland) Act 1971.

(2) The provisions of the Schedule to this Act of Sederunt shall not apply to a summary cause commenced before 30th November 1988.

3. Consequential amendment

[The amendment to para 3(1) of the Act of Sederunt (Summary Cause Rules, Sheriff Court) 1976 is included in the print of that Act, *supra.*]

Paragraph 2(1)   SCHEDULE

SMALL CLAIM RULES 1988

ARRANGEMENT OF RULES

PART I

INTRODUCTORY

PART II

RULES FOR SMALL CLAIMS FOR PAYMENT OF MONEY ONLY

Part III

Special Rules for Small Claims for Delivery or Recovery of Possession of Moveable Property and for Implement of an Obligation

PART I

INTRODUCTORY

1. Citation, application and interpretation

(1) These rules may be cited as the Small Claim Rules 1988.

(2) These rules shall apply to a small claim, being such summary cause proceedings as may be prescribed by the Lord Advocate under section 35(2) of the Sheriff Courts (Scotland) Act 1971.

(3) In these rules—

(a)   a form referred to by number means the form so numbered in Appendix 1 to these rules or a form substantially of the same effect with such variation as circumstances may require;

(b)   a reference to the Ordinary Cause Rules means the rules in Schedule 1 to the Sheriff Courts (Scotland) Act 1907; and

(c)   a reference to the Summary Cause Rules means the rules in the Schedule to the Act of Sederunt (Summary Cause Rules, Sheriff Court) 1976.

[1A. In these rules, unless the context otherwise requires, 'authorised lay representative' means a person to whom section 32(1) of the Solicitors (Scotland) Act 1980 (offence to prepare writs) does not apply by virtue of section 32(2)(a) of that Act.]

NOTE
Rule 1A: Inserted by SI 1991/821.

2. Application of certain Ordinary Cause, and Summary Cause, Rules

(1) The provisions of the Ordinary Cause Rules specified in Appendix 2 to these rules shall apply to a small claim insofar as not inconsistent with these rules.

(2) The provisions of the Summary Cause Rules specified in Appendix 3 to these rules shall apply to a small claim insofar as not inconsistent with these rules.

PART II

RULES FOR SMALL CLAIMS FOR PAYMENT OF MONEY ONLY

3.(1) A small claim for payment of money shall be commenced by summons in form 1.

(2) A service copy summons in form 2 shall be served on the defender in a small claim for payment of money only in which a time to pay direction may be applied for; and the small claim shall be subject to the rules in this Part.

(3) A service copy summons in form 3 shall be served on the defender in a small claim for payment of money only in which a time to pay direction may not be applied for; and the small claim shall be subject to the rules in this Part except rules 9 and 11 below.

(4) The pursuer shall give a statement of his claim in the summons to give the defender fair notice of the claim; and the statement shall include—

    (a)   details of the basis of the small claim including relevant dates;

[(b)   where the small claim arises from the supply of goods or services, a description of the goods or services and the date or dates on or between which they were supplied and, where relevant, ordered;]

    (c)   a reference to any agreement which the pursuer has reason to believe may exist giving jurisdiction over the subject matter of the small claim to another court;

    (d)   a reference to any proceedings which the pursuer has reason to believe may be pending before another court involving the same cause of action and between the same parties as those named in the summons.

(5) A summons shall be signed—

    (a)   by the sheriff clerk; or

    (b)   by the sheriff, if he thinks fit, where—

        (i)   the defender's address is unknown; or

        (ii)   the sheriff clerk has for any reason refused to sign the summons.

(6) The signed summons shall be warrant for service on the defender and, where the appropriate warrant has been included in the summons, warrant of arrestment on the dependence or for arrestment to found jurisdiction, as the case may be.

NOTE
Rule 3(4)(b): Substituted by SI 1992/249.

4.   Period of notice

(1) A small claim shall proceed after the appropriate period of notice of the summons has been given to the defender.

(2) The appropriate period of notice shall be—

    (a)   21 days where the defender is resident or has a place of business within Europe; or

    (b)   42 days where the defender is resident or has a place of business outwith Europe.

(3) Where a period of notice expires on a Saturday, Sunday, public or local holiday, the period of notice shall be deemed to expire on the first following day on which the sheriff clerk's office is open for civil court business.

[(4) Notwithstanding the terms of section 4(2) of the Citation Amendment (Scotland) Act 1882, where service is by post the period of notice shall run from the beginning of the day next following the date of posting.]

(5) The sheriff clerk shall insert in the summons the date which is at the end

of the period of notice being the last day on which the defender may return a response form to the sheriff clerk (the return date).

NOTE
Rule 4(4): Substituted by SI 1992/249.

---

5.   Service of summons where address of defender is known

(1) Subject to paragraph (7) of this rule, a service copy summons shall be served on the defender by the pursuer's solicitor, a sheriff officer or the sheriff clerk sending it by first class recorded delivery post, or by one of the methods specified in rule 6(1), (2) or (4) of the Summary Cause Rules (citation and service within Scotland by officer of court).

(2) Where the pursuer requires the sheriff clerk to effect service on his behalf by virtue of section 36A of the Sheriff Courts (Scotland) Act 1971 (pursuer not a partnership, body corporate or acting in a representative capacity), he may require the sheriff clerk to supply him with a copy of the summons.

(3) Subject to paragraph (7) of this rule, where service is to be effected by the sheriff clerk, he may do so by posting the service copy summons by first class recorded delivery post or, on payment to the sheriff clerk by the pursuer of the fee prescribed by the Secretary of State by order, by sheriff officer.

(4) There shall be enclosed with the service copy summons a form of service in form 4.

(5) On the face of the envelope used for postal service in terms of this rule there shall be printed or written a notice in form 5.

(6) A certificate of service in form 6 shall be attached to the summons after service has been effected under this rule.

(7) Service on a defender who is outwith Scotland shall be effected in the manner prescribed by rule 9 of the Summary Cause Rules (citation of or service on persons outside Scotland).

(8) Where service is to be effected by the sheriff clerk under paragraph (7), any cost occasioned thereby shall be borne by the pursuer and no such service shall be instructed by the sheriff clerk until payment of such cost has been made to him by the pursuer.

6.   Service where address of defender is unknown

(1) Where the defender's address is unknown to the pursuer, the sheriff may grant warrant to serve the summons—
   (a)   by the publication of an advertisement in form 7 in a newspaper circulating in the area of the defender's last known address; or
   (b)   by displaying on the walls of court a copy of a notice in form 8,
and the period of notice, which shall be fixed by the sheriff, shall run from the date of publication of the advertisement or display on the walls of court, as the case may be.

(2) Where service is to be effected under paragraph (1) of this rule, the pursuer shall lodge a service copy of the summons with the sheriff clerk from whom it may be uplifted by the defender.

(3) Where the pursuer requires the sheriff clerk to effect service on his behalf under paragraph (1) of this rule by virtue of section 36A of the Sheriff Courts (Scotland) Act 1971 (pursuer not a partnership, body corporate or acting in a representative capacity)—

    (a)   the cost of any advertisement required under paragraph (1)(a) of this rule shall be borne by the pursuer and no such advertisement shall be instructed by the sheriff clerk until such cost has been paid to him by the pursuer; and

    (b)   the pursuer may require the sheriff clerk to supply him with a copy of the summons.

(4) Where service by advertisement is made under paragraph (1)(a) of this rule, a copy of the newspaper containing the advertisement shall be lodged with the sheriff clerk unless advertisement is instructed by the sheriff clerk under paragraph (3) of this rule.

(5) Where display on the walls of court is required under paragraph (1)(b) of this rule, the pursuer shall supply to the sheriff clerk for that purpose a copy of form 8 duly completed unless service is to be effected by the sheriff clerk under paragraph (3) of this rule.

(6) Where service has been made under this rule and thereafter the defender's address becomes known, the sheriff may allow the summons to be amended and, if appropriate, grant warrant for re-service subject to such conditions as he thinks fit.

7. Return of summons

(1) Where service has been effected other than by the sheriff clerk, the pursuer shall return the summons with a certificate of service to the sheriff clerk on or before the return date, failing which the sheriff may dismiss the small claim.

(2) Where the summons has been served by the sheriff clerk, he shall intimate to the pursuer, forthwith after the return date, whether or not a response to the summons has been tendered by the defender; and such intimation shall be made by the sheriff clerk sending to the pursuer by first class recorded delivery post a copy of form 9 (claim admitted; payment by instalments or lump sum), 10 (no response) or 11 (claim admitted and defender to appear or claim not admitted or jurisdiction challenged), as appropriate.

8. Response to summons where defender intends to appear

(1) Where the defender intends—

    (a)   to challenge the jurisdiction of the court;

    (b)   to defend the small claim;

    (c)   to dispute the amount of the small claim; or

(d) to admit the small claim and make oral application for a time to pay direction (including, where appropriate, an application for recall or restriction of an arrestment),

he shall intimate his intention to appear by completing the appropriate part of the form of response attached to the service copy summons and shall lodge it with the sheriff clerk on or before the return date.

(2) A defender who intends to defend a small claim and has delivered a form of response to the sheriff clerk may, at any time prior to the date of the preliminary hearing of the small claim, lodge a written note of the defence which he proposes to state at the preliminary hearing.

(3) Where the defender has delivered a written note of this proposed defence to the small claim to the sheriff clerk, the defender shall, at the same time, send a copy of it to the pursuer.

9. Response to summons where defender does not intend to appear

Where the defender admits the small claim and does not intend to appear, he may, where competent, make an application for a time to pay direction (including, where appropriate, an application for recall or restriction of an arrestment) by completing the appropriate part of the form of response attached to the service copy summons and lodge it with the sheriff clerk on or before the return date.

10. No response by defender

(1) Where a form of response has not been lodged by the defender in accordance with rule 8 or 9 above, the cause shall not be called in court and, if before noon on the day prior to the date for the preliminary hearing, the pursuer, his solicitor or his solicitor's authorised clerk enters a minute in the Book of Small Claims or lodges form 10 with the minute in box 1 or 2 duly signed, or a minute in form 12, as the case may be, decree or other order in terms of that minute may be granted on the date for the preliminary hearing.

(2) Where the pursuer does not enter a minute in the Book of Small Claims or lodge form 10 with the minute in box 1 or 2 duly signed, or a minute in form 12 in accordance with paragraph (1) of this rule, the court shall dismiss the small claim.

(3) A decree granted under paragraph (1) of this rule shall be subject to recall in accordance with the provisions of rule 27 below.

(4) The sheriff shall not grant decree under paragraph (1) of this rule unless it is clear from the terms of the summons that a ground of jurisdiction exists.

11. Consent to application for time to pay direction

(1) Where the defender has delivered a form of response to the sheriff clerk in accordance with rule 9 above making application for a time to pay direction (including, where appropriate, an application for recall or restriction of an

arrestment), the pursuer may intimate that he does not object to the application by—
  (a)   entering a minute in the Book of Small Claims stating that he does not object to the defender's application and for decree;
  (b)   lodging with the sheriff clerk a minute in form 12; or
  (c)   lodging with the sheriff clerk form 9 with a minute duly signed,
before noon on the day prior to the date for the preliminary hearing.

(2) Where the pursuer intimates under paragraph (1) of this rule that he does not object to the defender's application for a time to pay direction (including, where appropriate, an application for recall or restriction of an arrestment), the sheriff may grant decree on the date for the preliminary hearing and the parties shall not be required to attend and the cause shall not be called, in court.

12.   Preliminary hearing

(1) A preliminary hearing shall be held where—
  (a)   the defender has intimated his intention to appear in accordance with rule 8(1) above; or
  (b)   the defender has made an application for a time to pay direction (including, where appropriate, an application for recall or restriction of an arrestment) in accordance with rule 9 above which the pursuer does not accept.

(2) The preliminary hearing shall be held seven days after the return date, and may be continued to such other date as the court shall consider appropriate.

(3) The sheriff clerk shall insert in the summons the date for the preliminary hearing.

(4) Where the defender has delivered a form of response to the sheriff clerk in accordance with rule 8(1)(a), (b) or (c) above, he shall attend or be represented at the preliminary hearing and state his defence to the court (which shall be noted by the sheriff on the summons).

(5) Where the defender has delivered a form of response to the sheriff clerk in accordance with rule 8(1)(d) above, he shall attend or be represented at the preliminary hearing and may make oral representations in support of his application.

(6) Where the defender has delivered a form of response to the sheriff clerk in accordance with rule 9 above which the pursuer has not accepted, the sheriff shall make such order on the defender's application as he considers appropriate.

13.   Conduct of preliminary hearing

(1) Subject to paragraph (2) of this rule, where the defender has delivered a form of response to the sheriff clerk in accordance with rule 8(1) above but does not appear and has not stated a defence, decree may be granted against the defender in terms of the summons.

(2) The sheriff shall not grant decree until paragraph (1) of this rule unless it is clear from the terms of the summons that a ground of jurisdiction exists.

(3) Where the pursuer does not appear or is not represented at the preliminary hearing at which the defender is present or represented and if a defence has not been stated, the court shall grant decree absolving the defender.

(4) Where, at the preliminary hearing, the sheriff is satisfied that the small claim is incompetent or that there is a patent defect of jurisdiction, he may grant decree of dismissal in favour of the defender.

(5) At the preliminary hearing, the sheriff shall ascertain from the parties or their representatives what the disputed issues in the small claim are and shall make a note of them on the summons; and it shall thereafter be unnecessary for a party to satisfy the sheriff on any issue which is not noted as a disputed issue.

(6) Where the sheriff is satisfied that the facts are sufficiently admitted, he may decide the small claim on the merits at the preliminary hearing and if appropriate make an award of expenses.

(7) If, at the preliminary hearing or at any subsequent state of the small claim, a disputed issue noted by the sheriff is the quality or condition of an object, the sheriff may inspect the object in the presence of the parties or their representatives in court or, if it is not practicable to bring the object to court, at the place where the object is located.

(8) The sheriff may, if he considers it appropriate, inspect any place material to the disputed issues in the presence of the parties or their representatives.

(9) The sheriff may, on the joint motion of the parties, if he considers it to be appropriate, remit to any suitable person to report on any matter of fact.

(10) Where a remit is made under paragraph (9) of this rule, the report of such person shall be final and conclusive with respect to the matter of fact which is the subject of the remit.

(11) A remit shall not be made under paragraph (9) of this rule unless parties have previously agreed the basis upon which the fees, if any, of such person shall be met by them.

(12) Where any issue of fact between the parties is still disputed, the sheriff shall appoint a date for a hearing.

14. Remit between rolls

(1) Where a direction has been made by the sheriff under section 37(2B) of the Sheriff Courts (Scotland) Act 1971 that a small claim be treated as a summary cause or as an ordinary cause, the small claim shall be remitted to the summary cause roll or ordinary cause roll, as the case may be, first occurring not sooner than seven days after the date of that direction.

(2) Where a direction has been made under section 37 of the Sheriff Courts (Scotland) Act 1971 that a summary cause or an ordinary cause be treated as a small claim, the initial writ or summary cause summons, as the case may be, shall be treated as a small claim summons and the cause shall be remitted to the small claim roll occurring not more than seven days after the date of the

direction; or, if there is no roll within that period, to the roll first occurring thereafter.

15. Alteration of summons, etc

The sheriff may, on the motion of a party, allow amendment of the summons, statement of claim or note of defence and adjust the disputed issues at any time.

16. Witnesses

(1) A party to a small claim shall be entitled to give and lead evidence but shall be responsible for securing the attendance of his witnesses at a hearing and shall be personally liable for their expenses (which shall form expenses in the cause only up to the limit prescribed in rule 26 below).

(2) The hearing of a small claim shall not be adjourned solely on account of the failure of a witness to appear unless the sheriff on cause shown so directs.

(3) Evidence by a party or witness shall be given on oath or affirmation.

17. Productions

(1) A party who intends to found at a hearing (other than a preliminary hearing) upon any documents or articles in his possession, which are reasonably capable of being lodged with the court, shall lodge them with the sheriff clerk together with a list detailing the items no later than seven days before the hearing and shall at the same time send a copy of the list to the other party.

(2) A party litigant [or an authorised lay representative] shall not borrow a production except with leave of the sheriff and subject to such conditions as the sheriff may impose, but may inspect them within the office of the sheriff clerk during normal business hours, and may obtain copies, where practicable, from the sheriff clerk.

(3) Only documents or articles—
(a)   produced in accordance under paragraph (1) of this rule;
(b)   produced at the preliminary hearing; or
(c)   produced under rule 18 below.
may be used or put in evidence, unless with the consent of the parties or the permission of the sheriff.

NOTE
Rule 17(2): Words added by SI 1991/821.

---

18. Recovery of documents

(1) Any party may apply to the sheriff for an order for recovery of such documents, referred to in a list of documents lodged by that party, as the sheriff considers relevant to the disputed issues.

(2) Where an order has been granted under paragraph (1) of this rule, a copy of it may be served by first class recorded delivery post on the person from whom the documents are sought to be recovered together with a certificate in form 13, and the order of the court shall be implemented in the manner and within the time specified in the order.

(3) Where the party in whose favour an order under paragraph (1) of this rule has been granted is not—

(a)   a partnership or body corporate; or

(b)   acting in a representative capacity,

and is not represented by a solicitor, service under paragraph (2) of this rule shall be effected by the sheriff clerk posting a copy of the order together with a certificate in form 13 by first class recorded delivery post or, on payment of the fee prescribed by the Secretary of State by order, by sheriff officer.

(4) Documents recovered in response to an order under paragraph (1) of this rule shall be sent to, and retained by, the sheriff clerk who shall, on receiving them, advise the parties that the documents are in his possession and (subject to rule 39 of the Summary Cause Rules (confidentiality)) may be examined within his office during normal business hours.

(5) In the event of a person, from whom documents are sought to be recovered, failing to implement an order of the court in the manner or within the time specified, the party seeking recovery may apply to the sheriff for an order requiring that person to appear before him to explain his failure; and if such person shall fail to appear he may be held in contempt of court.

(6) Documents recovered under this rule may be tendered as evidence at any hearing without further formality, and rule 17(2) above shall apply to such documents.

19.   Hearing

Any hearing, including a preliminary hearing, shall be conducted in public in such manner as the sheriff considers best suited to the clarification of the issue before him; and shall, so far as practicable, be conducted in an informal manner.

20.   Noting of evidence

The sheriff shall make notes of the evidence at a hearing for his own use and shall retain these notes until after any appeal has been disposed of.

21.   Documents, etc, referred to during hearing

Documents or other productions referred to during a hearing, and a report of a person to whom a matter has been remitted, shall be retained in the custody of the sheriff clerk until any appeal has been disposed of.

22. Abandonment of small claim

(1) At any time prior to decree being pronounced, the pursuer may offer to abandon the small claim.

(2) Where the pursuer offers to abandon, the sheriff clerk shall assess the sum of expenses payable by the pursuer to the defender calculated on such basis as the sheriff may direct (subject to section 36B of the Sheriff Courts (Scotland) Act 1971 and rule 26 below).

(3) The pursuer shall make payment to the defender of the assessed sum of expenses within 14 days of the date of assessment; and the court may thereafter dismiss the claim.

(4) Where the pursuer fails to make payment of the sum of assessed expenses within 14 days of the date of assessment, the court shall absolve the defender with expenses in favour of the defender.

23. Decree by default and dismissal

(1) Where, after a defence has been stated, a party fails to appear or be represented at any hearing, a special hearing shall be fixed by the court to be held not earlier than 14 days after the date of such failure.

(2) Where a special hearing is fixed by the court under paragraph (1) of this rule, the sheriff clerk shall forthwith—
- (a)   intimate the date, time and place of the special hearing to the party who has failed to appear or to be represented;
- (b)   advise him of the reason for the special hearing; and
- (c)   advise him that decree may be granted against him if—
  - (i)   he fails to appear or be represented at the special hearing; or
  - (ii)   at the special hearing good cause is not shown for non-appearance at any prior hearing.

(3) Where a party—
- (a)   fails to appear to be represented at a special hearing;
- (b)   fails to show cause at a special hearing for his non-appearance at a prior hearing; or
- (c)   fails to appear or be represented at any hearing after a special hearing,

decree by default or decree absolving the defender may be granted.

(4) Where, after a defence has been stated, a party fails to implement an order of the court, the sheriff may, after giving him an opportunity to be heard, grant decree by default or absolve the defender.

(5) Where all parties fail to appear or be represented at any hearing, the sheriff shall, unless sufficient reason appears to the contrary, dismiss the small claim.

24. Application for a time to pay direction in defended small claims

A defender in a small claim which proceeds as defended may, where it is competent to do so, make a written or oral application to the court, at any time before decree is granted, for a time to pay direction (including where appropriate, an order recalling or restricting an arrestment).

25. Decree

(1) The sheriff shall, where practicable, give his decision and a brief statement of his reasons at the conclusion of the hearing of a small claim or reserve judgment.

(2) Where the sheriff reserves judgment, he shall, within 28 days of the hearing give his decision in writing together with a brief note of his reasons; and the sheriff clerk shall forthwith intimate these to the parties.

(3) After giving his judgment, the sheriff shall—
  (a)   deal with the question of expenses and, where appropriate, make an award of expenses; and
  (b)   grant decreee as appropriate,

(4) A decree of the sheriff in a small claim shall be a final decree.

26. Expenses

[Subject to section 36B of the Sheriff Courts (Scotland) Act 1971 and to paragraph 4 of the Small Claims (Scotland) Order 1988, rule 88 (expenses) of the Summary Cause Rules shall apply to the determination of an award of expenses in a small claim as it applies to the determination of such an award in a summary cause.]

NOTE
Rule 26: Submitted by SI 1991/821.

---

27. Recall of decree

(1) A pursuer, at any time within 21 days of the grant of decree absolving the defender under rule 13(3) above, may apply for the recall of that decree by lodging with the sheriff clerk a minute for recall of the decree in form 14.

(2) A defender, at any time not later than 14 days after the execution of a charge or execution of arrestment, whichever first occurs, following on the grant of decree in terms of rule 10(1) or 13(1) above, may apply for the recall of that decree by lodging with the sheriff clerk a minute for recall of the decree in form 14.

(3) A party may apply for recall of a decree in the same small claims on one occasion only.

(4) Where the party seeking recall of a decree is not—
  (a)   a partnership or a body corporate; or
  (b)   acting in a representative capacity,
and is not represented by a solicitor, the sheriff clerk shall assist that party to complete and lodge a minute for recall of the decree.

(5) . . .

(6) On the lodging of a minute for recall of a decree, the sheriff clerk shall fix a date, time and place for a hearing of the minute; and a copy of the minute together with a note of the date, time and place of the hearing shall be served upon the other party not less than seven days before the date fixed for the hearing by the party seeking recall.

(7) Where the party seeking recall is not—

(a) a partnership or body corporate; or

(b) acting in a representative capacity,

and is not represented by a solicitor, service of the minute shall be effected by the sheriff clerk either by first class recorded delivery post or, on payment of the fee prescribed by the Secretary of State by order, by sheriff officer.

(8) At a hearing under paragraph (6) of this rule, the sheriff shall recall the decree so far as not implemented; and the small claim shall proceed in all respects as if the hearing were a preliminary hearing.

(9) . . .

(10) A minute for recall of a decree, when duly lodged and served in terms of this rule, shall have the effect of preventing any further action being taken by the other party to enforce the decree.

(11) On service of the copy minute for recall of a decree, any party in possession of the summon shall return it to the sheriff clerk.

NOTE

Sub-paras (5), (9): Revoked by SI 1990/2105.

---

28. Book of Small Claims

(1) The sheriff clerk shall keep a book to be known as the Book of Small Claims in which shall be entered a note of all small claims, minutes under rule 27 above (recall of decree) and minutes under rule 92(1) of the Summary Cause Rules (applications in same cause for variation etc of decree), setting forth, where appropriate—

(a) the names, designations and addresses of the parties;

(b) whether the parties were present or absent at any hearing, including an inspection, and the names of their representatives;

(c) the nature of the cause;

(d) the amount of any claim;

(e) the date of issue of the summons;

(f) the method of service;

(g) the return date;

(h) whether a form of response was lodged, and details thereof;

(i) whether a statement of defence was lodged;

(j) details of any minute by the pursuer intimating that he does not object to an application for a time to pay direction, or minute by the pursuer requesting decree or other order;

(k) details of any interlocutors issued;

(l) details of the final decree and the date thereof; and

   (m)   details of any variation or recall of a decree by virtue of the Debtors (Scotland) Act 1987.

   (2) The Book of Small Claims shall be signed in respect of each court day by the sheriff.

   (3) The book of Small Claims may be made up of separate rolls, each roll relating solely to proceedings of a particular description of small claim.

   (4) The Book of Small Claims shall be open for inspection during normal business hours.

29. Appeals

(1) An appeal to the sheriff principal, other than an appeal to which rule 85A of the Summary Cause Rules (appeals in relation to time to pay directions) applies, shall be by note of appeal—
   (a)   requesting a stated case;
   (b)   specifying the point of law upon which the appeal is to proceed; and
   (c)   lodged with the sheriff clerk not later than 14 days after the date of final decree.

   (2) The appellant shall, at the same time as lodging a note of appeal, intimate its lodging to the other party.

   (3) The sheriff shall, within 14 days of the lodging a note of appeal, issue a draft stated case containing—
   (a)   findings in fact and law or, where appropriate, a narrative of the proceedings before him;
   (b)   appropriate questions of law; and
   (c)   a note stating the reasons for his decision in law,
and the sheriff clerk shall send a copy of the draft stated case to the parties.

   (4) Within 14 days of the issue of the draft stated case—
   (a)   a party may lodge with the sheriff clerk a note of any adjustments which he seeks to make;
   (b)   the respondent may state any point of law which he wishes to raise in the appeal; and
   (c)   the note of adjustment and, where appropriate, point of law shall be intimated to the other party.

   (5) The sheriff may, on the motion of a party or of his own accord [and shall where he proposes to reject any proposed adjustment] allow a hearing on adjustments and may provide for such further procedure under this rule prior to the hearing of the appeal as he thinks fit.

   (6) The sheriff shall, within 14 days after—
   (a)   the latest date on which a note of adjustment has been or may be lodged; or
   (b)   where there has been a hearing on adjustments, that hearing,
and after considering such note and any representations made to him at the hearing, state and sign the case.

   [(6A) Where the sheriff is temporarily absent from duty for any reason, the sheriff principal may extend any period specified in paragraphs (3) or (6) for such period or periods as he considers reasonable.]

(7) The stated case signed by the sheriff shall include questions of law, framed by him, arising from the points of law stated by the parties and such other questions of laws as he may consider appropriate.

(8) After the sheriff has signed the stated case, the sheriff clerk shall—

(a)   place before the sheriff principal all documents and productions in the small claim together with the stated case; and

(b)   send to the parties a copy of the stated case together with a written note of the date, time and place of the hearing of the appeal.

(9) In the hearing of an appeal, a party shall not be allowed to raise questions of law of which notice has not been given except on cause shown and subject to such condition as to expenses or otherwise as the sheriff principal may consider appropriate.

NOTE
Rule 29(5): Words inserted by SI 1992/249.
Rule 29(6A): Sub-para inserted by SI 1992/249.

30.   Representation

[(1) A party may be represented by an advocate, solicitor or, subject to the following provisions of this rule, an authorised lay representative.

(2) Subject to the following provisions of this rule, an authorised lay representative may in representing a party do all such things for the preparation and conduct of a small claim as may be done by an individual conducting his own claim.

(3) An authorised lay representative shall cease to represent a party if the sheriff finds either that the authorised lay representative is not a suitable person to represent the party or that he is not authorised to do so.]

NOTE
Rule 30: Substituted by SI 1991/821.

31.   Application of rules to solicitors

Where a rule requires something to be done by, or intimated or sent to, a party, it shall be sufficient compliance with the rule if it is done by, or intimated or sent to, the solicitor acting for that party in the small claim.

32.   Contents of envelope containing service copy summons

A document not forming part of the summons or any form of response or other notice in accordance with these rules shall not be included in the same envelope as the service copy summons.

33. Incidental applications

(1) Except where otherwise provided, any incidental application in a small claim shall be lodged with the sheriff clerk and shall only be heard after two days' notice has been given to the other party.

(2) A party who is not—

(a)   a partnership or a body corporate; or

(b)   acting in a representative capacity,

and is not represented by a solicitor, may require the sheriff clerk to intimate to the other party a copy of an incident application.

(3) The sheriff clerk shall keep a book to be known as the Book of Incidental Applications in Small Claims in which shall be entered all applications incidental to a small claim, other than minutes under rule 10(1), 11(1) or 27(1) above or under rule 92(1) of the Summary Cause Rules (applications in same cause for variation etc of decree), and in which shall be set forth the following particulars, where appropriate—

(a)   the names of the parties together with a clear reference to the entry in the Book of Small Claims;

(b)   whether parties are present or absent at the hearing of the application, and the names of their representatives;

(c)   the nature of the application; and

(d)   the interlocutor issued or order made.

(4) The Book of Incidental Applications in Small Claims shall be—

(a)   signed by the sheriff on each day on which incidental applications are heard; and

(b)   be open for inspection during normal business hours to all concerned without fee.

34. Dispensing power of sheriff

The sheriff may relieve any party from the consequences of any failure to comply with the provisions of these rules which is shown to be due to mistake, oversight or other cause, not being wilful non-observance of the rules, on such terms and conditions as seem just; and in any such case the sheriff may make such order as seems just by way of extension of time, lodging or amendment of papers or otherwise so as to enable the small claim to proceed as if such failure had not occurred.

PART III

SPECIAL RULES FOR SMALL CLAIMS FOR DELIVERY OR RECOVERY OF POSSESSION OR MOVEABLE PROPERTY AND FOR IMPLEMENT OF AN OBLIGATION

35. Application

(1) The provisions of Part II of these rules shall apply to a small claim for

which rules are provided in this Part, except insofar as those provisions are inconsistent with the rules in this Part.

(2) The provisions of this Part of these rules shall apply to a small claim for delivery or recovery of possession of moveable property or for implement of an obligation to which article 2(b) or 3 of the Small Claims (Scotland) Order 1988 applies.

36. Summons for delivery or recovery of possession of moveable property

(1) A small claim for delivery or recovery of possession of moveable property shall be commenced by summons in form 15.

(2) A service copy summons in form 16 shall be served on the defender in a small claim for delivery or recovery of possession of moveable property in which a time to pay direction may be applied for.

(3) A service copy summons in form 17 shall be served on the defender in a small claim for delivery or recovery of possession of moveable property in which a time to pay direction may not be applied for.

37. Summons for implement of an obligation

(1) A small claim for implement of an obligation shall be commenced by summons in form 18.

(2) A service copy summons in form 19 shall be served on the defender in a small claim for implement of an obligation in which a time to pay direction may be applied for.

(3) A service copy summons in form 20 shall be served on the defender in a small claim for implement of an obligation in which a time to pay direction may not be applied for.

38. Service

(1) Where service of the copy summons has been effected other than by the sheriff clerk, the pursuer shall return the summons together with a certificate of service in form 6 to the sheriff clerk at least 24 hours before the date of the preliminary hearing.

(2) Where paragraph (1) of this rule is not complied with, the sheriff may dismiss the small claim.

39. Time to pay directions

(1) In a small claim where a service copy summons has been served under rule 36(2) or 37(2) above, the defender may, if he does not intend to defend, apply for a time to pay direction, where it is competent to do so, by—
    (a)   appearing at the preliminary hearing and making a motion for a time to pay direction; or

(b)   completing and returning to the sheriff clerk, at least seven days before the date specified in the service copy summons for the preliminary hearing, the appropriate portion of form 16 or 19, as the case may be.

(2) In a small claim where a service copy summons has been served under rule 36(2) or 37(2) above which proceeds as defended, the defender may, where it is competent to do so, apply for a time to pay direction by written or oral application to the court at any time before final decree is granted.

(3) Where a defender applies for a time to pay direction under this rule, he may at the same time apply for an order recalling or restricting an arrestment on the dependence of the action or in security of the sum concerned by completing and delivery to the sheriff clerk the appropriate part of form 16 or 19, as the case may be.

40.   Preliminary hearing

(1) A preliminary hearing shall be held on the date specified in the summons.

(2) Where the defender does not appear or is not represented at the preliminary hearing, decree may be granted against him.

41.   Decree for alternative claim for payment

(1) Where decree for delivery or recovery of possession or moveable property or for implement of an obligation has been granted but the defender has failed to comply with that decree, the pursuer may lodge with the sheriff clerk an incidental application of decree in terms of the alternative crave for payment: and the incidental application shall be intimated to the defender.

(2) The pursuer shall appear at the hearing of an incidental application under paragraph (1) of this rule.

Rule 2(1)   APPENDIX 2

RULES FOR ORDINARY CAUSE RULES WHICH APPLY TO
SMALL CLAIMS

[APPENDIX 2

rule 5.7 (persons carrying on business under trading or descriptive name),
rule 6.1 (service of schedule of arrestment),
rule 12.2(2) (correction of clerical errors in interlocutors)
rule 25.1 (minutes of sist),
rule 25.2 (minutes of transference),
rule 28.14 (letters of request),
rule 30.2 (taxes on money under control of the court)
rule 30.9 (service of charge where address of defender not known),
rules 36.14 to 36.17 (management of damages payable to persons under legal disability),

Chapter 38 (European Court).]

NOTE
Appendix 2: Substituted by SI 1993/1956 in relation to causes commenced on or after 1 January 1994.

Rule 2(2)   APPENDIX 3

RULES OF THE SUMMARY CAUSE RULES WHICH APPLY TO
SMALL CLAIMS

rule 3A (information on summons).
rule 6(1), (2) and (4) (citation and service within Scotland by officer of the court).
rule 9 (citation of or service on persons outwith Scotland).
rule 11 (endorsation of summons by sheriff clerk of defender's residence not necessary).
rule 12 (re-service).
rule 13 (defender appearing barred from objecting to citation).
rule 18(8) (sheriff to be satisfied that defender outwith Scotland also to receive summons).
rule 18A (decree in causes to which the Hague Convention applies).
[**rule 21A** (party minuter).]
rule 22 (transfer to another court).
rule 24A(1) and (2) (borrowing of productions).
rule 26 (documents lost or destroyed).
rule 29 (citation of witnesses).
rule 30 (form of citation and execution thereof).
rule 31 (failure to answer citation).
rule 32 (witnesses failing to attend).
rule 39 (confidentiality).
rule 47 (arrestment).
rule 48 (recall and restriction of arrestment).
rule 71 (diligence of decree in action of delivery).
rule 82 (effect of and abandonment of appeal).
rule 83(1), (3) and (4) (hearing of appeal).
rule 85 (sheriff to regulate interim possession).
rule 85A (appeal in relation to time to pay direction).
rule 89 (extract of decree).
rule 92 (applications in same cause for variation, etc, of decree).
form N (citation of witness).
form O (execution of citation of witness).
forms U1, U2, U2A, U9, U10, U11, U13 and U14 (extract decrees).

NOTE
Appendix 3: Words inserted by SI 1992/249.

Ordinary Cause Rules 1993

Applying to small claims

5.7. Persons carrying on business under trading or descriptive name

(1) A person carrying on a business under a trading or descriptive name may sue or be sued in such trading or descriptive name alone; and an extract—

   (a) of a decree pronounced in the sheriff court, or

   (b) of a decree proceeding upon any deed, decree arbitral, bond, protest of a bill, promissory note or banker's note or upon any other obligation or document on which execution may proceed, recorded in the sheriff court books against such person under such trading or descriptive name,

shall be a valid warrant for diligence against such person.

(2) An initial writ, decree, charge, warrant or any other order or writ following upon such initial writ or decree in a cause in which a person carrying on business under a trading or descriptive name sues or is sued in that name may be served—

   (a) at any place of business or office at which such business is carried on within the sheriffdom of the sheriff court in which the cause is brought; or

   (b) where there is no place of business within the sheriffdom, at any place where such business is carried on (including the place of business or office of the clerk or secretary of any company, corporation or association or firm).

25.1. Minutes of sist

Where a party dies or comes under legal incapacity while a cause is depending, any person claiming to represent that party or his estate may apply by minute to be sisted as a party to the cause.

25.2. Minutes of transference

(1) Where a party dies or comes under legal incapacity while a cause is depending and the provisions of rule 25.1 are not invoked, any other party may apply by minute to have that cause transferred in favour of or against, as the cause may be, any person who represents that party or his estate.

(2) The party intimating a minute of transference on a person referred to in paragraph (1) of this rule in accordance with rule 15.2 by virtue of rule 14.3(5) (intimation of minutes) shall at the same time intimate a copy of the pleadings (including any adjustments and amendments) to that person.

Summary Cause Rules 1976

Applying to small claims

[3A. Information on summons

The name and address of the pursuer's solicitor (if any) shall be entered by the solicitor on the principal summons, and the service document or service copy.]

NOTE
Rule 3A added by SI 1980/455.

[6. Citation and service within Scotland by officer of court

(1) Any summons, decree, charge, warrant or other order or writ following upon such summons or decree issued in a summary cause may be validly served by an officer of court [on any person],
   (a) by being served personally . . ., or
   (b) by being left in the hands of an inmate at the [person's] dwelling place or of an employee at the [person's] place of business.
   (2) Where an officer of court has been unsuccessful in effecting service in accordance with paragraph (1), he may, after making diligent inquiries, serve the said summons, decree, charge, warrant or other order or writ,
   (a) by depositing it in the [person's] dwelling place or place of business by means of a letter box or by other lawful means, or
   (b) by affixing it to the door of the [person's] dwelling place or place of business.
[Subject to the requirements of rule 111 of the rules contained in Schedule 1 to the Act of 1907, if] . . . in accordance with this paragraph, the officer shall thereafter send by ordinary post to the address at which he thinks it most likely that the [person] may be found, a letter containing a copy of any summons, decree, charge, warrant or other order or writ.
   (3) In proceedings in or following on a summary cause it shall be necessary for any officer of court to be accompanied by a witness except where service, citation or intimation is to be made by post.
   (4) In this rule 'officer of court' includes a sheriff officer but not a messenger-at-arms.]

NOTES
Rule 6 substituted by SI 1980/455.
Sub-paras (1) and (2) amended by SI 1992/249.

[9.   Citation of or service on persons outwith Scotland

(1) Subject to the following provisions of this rule, any summons or decree, or any other writ or order following upon such summons or decree, or any charge or warrant, may be served outwith Scotland on any person—

    (a)   at a known residence or place of business in England and Wales, Northern Ireland, the Isle of Man, the Channel Islands or any country with which the United Kingdom does not have a convention providing for service of writs in that country—

        (i)   in accordance with the rules for personal service under the domestic law of the place in which service is to be effected; or

        (ii)   by posting in Scotland a copy of the document in question in a registered or recorded delivery letter or the nearest equivalent which the available postal services permit addressed to the person at his residence or place of business;

    (b)   in a country which is a party to the Hague Convention on the Service Abroad of Judicial and Extra-Judicial Documents in Civil or Commercial Matters dated 15th November 1965 or the European Convention on Jurisdiction and Enforcement of Judgments in Civil and Commercial Matters as set out in Schedule 1 to the Civil Jurisdiction and Judgments Act 1982—

        (i)   by a method prescribed by the internal law of the country where service is to be effected for the service of documents in domestic actions upon persons who are within its territory;

        (ii)   by or through a central authority in the country where service is to be effected at the request of the Foreign Office;

        (iii)   by or through a British Consular authority at the request of the Foreign Office;

        (iv)   where the law of the country in which the person resides permits, by posting in Scotland a copy of the document in a registered or recorded delivery letter or the nearest equivalent which the available postal services permit addressed to the person at his residence; or

        (v)   where the law of the country in which service is to be effected permits, service by an *huissier*, other judicial officer or competent official of the country where service is to be made;

    (c)   in a country with which the United Kingdom has a convention on the service of writs in that country other than the conventions in subparagraph (b), by one of the methods approved in the relevant convention.

(2) A document which requires to be posted in Scotland for the purposes of this rule shall be posted by a solicitor or an officer of court, and the forms for citation and certificate of citation in rule 5 shall apply to a postal citation under this rule as they apply to a citation under that rule.

(3) On the face of the envelope used for postal service under this rule there shall be written or printed a notice in the same or similar terms as that required in the case of ordinary service under rule 10.

(4) Where service is effected by a method specified in paragraph (1)(b)(ii) or (iii), the pursuer shall—

(a)   send a copy of the summons and warrant for service with citation attached, or other document, with a request for service to be effected by the method indicated in the request to the Secretary of State for Foreign and Commonwealth Affairs; and

(b)   lodge in process a certificate of execution of service signed by the authority which has effected service.

(5) Where service is effected by the method specified in paragraph (1)(b)(v) the pursuer, his solicitor or the officer of court, shall—

(a)   send to the official in the country in which service is to be effected a copy of the summons and warrant for service, with citation attached, or other document, with a request for service to be effected by delivery to the defender or his residence; and

(b)   the pursuer shall lodge in process a certificate of execution of service by the official who has effected service.

(6) Where service is effected in accordance with paragraph (1)(a)(i) or (1)(b)(i), the pursuer shall lodge a certificate by a person who is conversant with the law of the country concerned and who practises or has practised as an advocate or solicitor in that country or is a duly accredited representative of the Government of that country, stating that the form of service employed is in accordance with the law of the place where the service was effected. It shall not be necessary to lodge such a certificate where service has taken place in another part of the United Kingdom, the Channel Isles or the Isle of Man.

(7) Every summons or document and every citation and notice on the face of the envelope referred to in paragraph (3) shall be accompanied by a translation in an official language of the country in which service is to be executed unless English is an official language of that country.

(8) A translation referred to in paragraph (7) shall be certified as a correct translation by the person making it and the certificate shall contain full name, address and qualifications of the translator and be lodged along with the execution of such citation or certificate of execution.]

NOTE
Rule 9 substituted by SI 1986/1946.

[11.   Endorsation of summons by sheriff clerk of defender's residence not necessary

Any summons, charge, warrant, arrestment or any order or writ following upon a summons or decree may be served, enforced or otherwise lawfully executed in Scotland without endorsation by a sheriff clerk and, if executed by an officer, may be so executed by an officer of the court which granted the summons, or by an officer of the sheriff court district in which it is to be executed.]

NOTE
Rule 11 substituted by SI 1980/455.

12. Re-service

(1) If it appears to the court that there has been any failure or irregularity in service upon a defender, the court may [prior to or at the first calling and] upon such conditions as seem just authorise the pursuer to reserve the summons.

(2) Where re-service has been ordered in accordance with paragraph (1) or rule 8 the cause shall proceed thereafter as if it were a new cause.

NOTE
Amended by SI 1978/1805.

13. Defender appearing barred from objecting to citation

Except where jurisdiction has been constituted by arrestment to found jurisdiction a party who appears or is represented may not object to the regularity of the service and the appearance shall be deemed to remedy any defect in the service.

. . .

[15. Return of summons

(1) In an action for payment of money to which [rules 50 to 55] apply the summons, together with the relevant certificate of citation shall be returned to the sheriff clerk on or before the return day referred to in rule 51.

(2) In all other actions, the summons together with the relevant certificate of citation shall be returned to the sheriff clerk at least 24 hours before the date of the first calling as defined in rule 18(1).

(3) Failure to comply with either paragraph (1) or (2) may result in the dismissal of the cause.]

NOTES
Rule 15 substituted by SI 1980/455.
Sub-para (1) amended by SI 1988/1978.

18. First calling

. . .

[(8) In the case of a defender domiciled in another part of the United Kingdom or in another Contracting State, the sheriff shall not grant decree in absence until it has been shown that the defender has been able to receive the summons in sufficient time to arrange for his defence or that all necessary steps have been taken to that end; and for the purposes of this paragraph—

    (a)   the question as to whether a person is domiciled in another part of the United Kingdom shall be determined in accordance with sections 41 and 42 of the Civil Jurisdiction and Judgments Act 1982;

(b) the question as to whether a person is domiciled in another Contracting State shall be determined in accordance with Article 52 of Schedule 1 to that Act; and

(c) the term 'Contracting State' has the meaning assigned to it by section 1 of that Act.]

NOTE
Sub-para (8) added by SI 1986/1946.

[18A. Decree in causes to which the Hague Convention applies

Where, in any civil proceedings (including proceedings for aliment), the summons has been served in a country to which the Hague Convention on the Service Abroad of Judicial and Extra-Judicial Documents in Civil or Commercial Matters dated 15th November 1965 applies, decree shall not be granted until it is established to the satisfaction of the sheriff that the requirements of Article 15 of that Convention have been complied with.]

NOTE
Rule 18A added by SI 1986/1946.

22. Transfer to another court

A cause may be transferred to any other court, whether in the same sheriffdom or not, if the sheriff considers that it is expedient that this be done and a cause so transferred shall proceed in all respects as if it had originally been brought in that court.

[24A. Borrowing of productions

(1) Any productions borrowed, receipts for which shall be entered in the inventory of productions, which inventory shall be retained by the sheriff clerk, shall be returned not later than noon on the day preceding the date of the proof.

(2) Productions may be borrowed only by a solicitor or by his duly authorised clerk for whom he shall be responsible.

(3) A party litigant [or authorised by representative] shall not borrow productions except by leave of the sheriff and subject to such conditions as the sheriff may impose, but may inspect them and obtain copies, where practicable, from the sheriff clerk.]

NOTES
Rule 24A added by SI 1980/455.
Sub-para (3) amended by SI 1991/821.

26. Documents lost or destroyed

When any summons, statement of claim, counter claim or note of defence, any book or document recording interlocutors or deliverances of the court or any document lodged with the sheriff clerk in connection with a summary cause is lost or destroyed, a copy thereof, authenticated in such manner as the sheriff may require, may be substituted and shall, for the purposes of the cause, including the use of diligence, be equivalent to the original.

29. Citation of witnesses

The summons or the copy served on the defender shall be sufficient warrant for the citation of witnesses and havers, the period of notice required to be given to such witnesses or havers being not less than seven days.

30. Form of citation and execution thereof

The citation of a witness or haver shall be in form N and the certificate thereof shall be in form O and a solicitor who cites a witness or haver shall be personally liable for the fees of the witness or haver.

31. Failure to answer citation

A witness or haver who fails to answer a citation after having been properly cited and offered his travelling expenses if he has asked for them may be ordered by the sheriff to pay a penalty not exceeding [£250] unless a reasonable excuse is offered and sustained. The sheriff may grant decree for payment of the said penalty in favour of the party on whose behalf the witness or haver was cited.

NOTE
Amended by SI 1992/249.

[32. Witnesses failing to attend

The sheriff may grant warrant to compel the attendance of a witness or haver under pain of arrest and imprisonment until caution can be found as the sheriff may require for his due attendance. The warrant shall be effective in any sheriffdom without endorsation and the expenses thereof may be awarded against the witness or haver.]

NOTE
Rule 32 substituted by SI 1980/455.

[39. Confidentiality

In any cause in which, either under the optional procedure provided in rule 38 or in the execution of a commission and diligence in normal form, confidentiality is claimed for any of the documents produced or where an order having been made under rule 68(c)(i) in the Schedule to the Act of 1907 confidentiality is claimed for any of the documents or other property produced, such documents or property shall be enclosed in a separate sealed packet, which shall not be opened or put in process except by authority of the sheriff obtained on the application of the party serving the order, or executing the commission and diligence, after opportunity has been given to the party, parties or haver, making production, to be heard.]

NOTE
Rule 39 substituted by SI 1980/455.

47. Arrestment

An arrestment to found jurisdiction or an arrestment on the dependence of an action used prior to service shall fall, unless the summons shall have been served within 42 days from the date of execution of the arrestment. When such an arrestment has been executed, the party using it or his solicitor shall forthwith report the execution to the sheriff clerk the certificate of excecution being on the same paper as the summons.

[48. Recall and restriction of arrestment

(1) A party may have an arrestment on the dependence of a cause loosed on paying into court, or finding caution to the satisfaction of the sheriff clerk in respect of, the sum claimed together with the sum of £50 in respect of expenses.

(2) On payment into court or the finding of caution to his satisfaction in accordance with paragraph (1), the sheriff clerk shall issue to the party a certificate which shall operate as a warrant for the release of any sum or property arrested and shall send a copy of the certificate to the party who instructed the arrestment.

(3) A party may at any time apply to the sheriff, duly intimated to the party who instructed the arrestment to recall or restrict an arrestment on the dependence of a cause, with or without consignation or caution.

(4) Where an application under paragraph (3) is granted, the sheriff clerk shall, when any condition imposed by the sheriff has been complied with, issue to the applicant a certificate which shall operate as a warrant for the release of any sum or property arrested to the extent ordered by the sheriff.]

NOTE
Rule 48 substituted by SI 1992/249.

[71. Diligence of decree

In an action for delivery the court may, when granting decree, grant warrant to search for and take possession of goods and to open shut and lockfast places. This warrant shall only apply to premises occupied by the defender and may only be executed after the expiry of a charge following upon the decree for delivery.]

82. Effect of and abandonment of appeal

When a note of appeal has been lodged it shall be available to and may be insisted on by all other parties in the cause notwithstanding that they may not have lodged separate appeals. After a note of appeal has been lodged, the appellant shall not be at liberty to withdraw it without the consent of the other parties which may be incorporated in a joint minute or by leave of the sheriff principal and on such terms as to expenses or otherwise as to him seems proper.

[83. Hearing of appeal

(1) The sheriff principal shall hear the parties or their solicitors orally on all matters connected with the appeal including liability for expenses: but if any party moves that the question of liability for expenses be heard after the sheriff principal has given his decision the sheriff principal may grant that motion.
    (2) The sheriff principal may permit a party to amend any question of law or to add any new question in accordance with rule 81(4).
    (3) The sheriff principal may—
    (a)   adhere to or vary the decree appealed against; or
    (b)   recall the decree appealed against and substitute another therefor; or
    (c)   remit, if he considers it desirable, to the sheriff, for any reason other than to have further evidence led.
    (4) At the conclusion of the hearing the sheriff principal may either pronounce his decision or reserve judgment in which latter case he shall within 28 days thereof give his decision in writing and the sheriff clerk shall forthwith intimate it to the parties.]

NOTE
Rule 83 substituted by SI 1980/455.

85. Sheriff to regulate interim possession

Notwithstanding an appeal the sheriff shall have power to regulate all matters relating to interim possession, to make any order for the preservation of any property to which the action relates or for its sale, if perishable, or for the preservation of evidence, or to make in his discretion any interim order which a due regard for the interests of the parties may require. Such orders shall not be subject to review except by the appellate court at the hearing of the appeal.

[85A. Appeal in relation to a time to pay direction

(1) This rule applies to appeals to the sheriff principal or to the Court of Session which relate solely to any application in connection with a time to pay direction.

(2) Rules 81, 81A, 82, 83(2) and 84 shall not apply to appeals under this rule.

(3) An application for leave to appeal against a decision in an application for a time to pay direction or any order connected therewith shall be made in writing, within seven days of that decision, to the sheriff who made the decision and shall specify the question of law upon which the appeal is to proceed.

(4) Where leave to appeal is granted, the appeal shall be lodged and intimated by the appellant to the other party within 14 days of the order granting leave and the sheriff shall state in writing his reasons for his original decision.

(5) An appeal to the sheriff principal shall proceed in accordance with paragraphs (1), (3) and (4) [of] rule 83.

(6) In an appeal to the Court of Session from the sheriff or the sheriff principal—
- (a) there shall be specified in the appeal the name and address of the solicitor in Edinburgh who will be acting for the appellant; and
- (b) the sheriff clerk shall transmit within four days to the Deputy Principal Clerk of Session—
  - (i) all documents and productions in the case;
  - (ii) a certified copy of the final decree;
  - (iii) the application for leave to appeal and the decision thereon;
  - (iv) the note of appeal;
  - (v) the sheriff's statement of reasons and, where appropriate, the sheriff principal's decision,

  all of which shall be deemed to be the sheriff court process.

(7) Within the period of four days mentioned in paragraph (6)(b), the sheriff clerk shall send written notice of the appeal to the other party and a certificate of intimation of written notice of the appeal shall be appended by him to the note of appeal.]

NOTE
Rule 85A added by SI 1988/1978.

89. Extract of decree

(1) Extract of a decree signed by the sheriff clerk may be issued only after the lapse of 14 days from the granting of the decree: Provided that [in actions

other than actions to which rule 68A] applies if an appeal has been lodged the extract may not be issued until the appeal has been disposed of.

(2) The extract decree which may be written on the summons or on a separate paper may be in one of the forms U1 to U14 and shall be warrant for all lawful diligence proceeding thereon.

NOTE
Sub-para (1) amended by SI 1980/455.

92. Applications in same cause for variation, etc, of decree

(1) Where by virtue of any enactment the sheriff, without a new summary cause being initiated, may order—
  (a)   a decree granted in a summary cause to be varied, discharged or rescinded, or
  (b)   the execution of that decree in so far as it has not already been executed to be sisted or suspended
the party requesting the court to make such an order shall do so by lodging a minute to that effect.

(2) On the lodging of such a minute by the pursuer in a summary cause the sheriff clerk shall grant warrant to cite the defender:
Provided that the pursuer has returned the summons and extract decree in the summary cause.

(3) On the lodging of such a minute by the defender in the summary cause the sheriff clerk shall grant warrant to cite the pursuer ordaining him to return the summons and extract decree in the summary cause and may, where appropriate, grant interim sist of execution of the decree.

(4) The minute shall be heard in court only when seven days' notice of the minute and warrant has been given;
  Provided that the sheriff may on cause shewn, alter the said period to there being a minimum period of two days.

[(5) This rule shall not apply to any proceedings under the Debtors (Scotland) Act 1987 or to proceedings which may be subject to the provisions of that Act.]

NOTE
Sub-para (5) added by SI 1988/1978.

INDEX

ST